I have a rule that goes like this: … Motyer is worth reading. *Cove*… exception to that rule. As Sincl… Motyer is doing 'covenant-center… theology.' If you want to learn from the Scriptures about the promise-keeping God, and how he pledges himself to a total work of salvation, then you have to study God's covenants. And here Alec Motyer clearly, simply, and helpfully walks you through Scripture tracing out how God makes and keeps his promises in his covenants.

LIGON DUNCAN
Chancellor and CEO, Reformed Theological Seminary,
Jackson, Mississippi

Motyer shows his readers the seamless unity of God's redeeming work across the Old Testament and into the New Testament. His attention to the connections between the Abrahamic Covenant and the Mosaic Covenant, in particular, are very clarifying. This work certainly will introduce many to a lifelong study of covenant theology and fuel their praise of our covenant God.

STEPHEN G. MYERS
Professor of Systematic and Historical Theology,
Puritan Reformed Theological Seminary;
Author of *God to Us: Covenant Theology in Scripture*

Somehow, some years back, I happened on to Alec Motyer's 'Covenant Theology' lectures—they were produced by the Theological Students Fellowship in thin yellow paper covers and mimeographed in blue ink. They got terribly marked up—there were so many of those 'Yes, oh, I see it now' moments. This is all vintage Alec—clear, warm, stimulating, whimsical, God-exposing. If you want to understand and enjoy the Bible, read this book.

Dale Ralph Davis

Author of *My Exceeding Joy: Psalm 38-51*

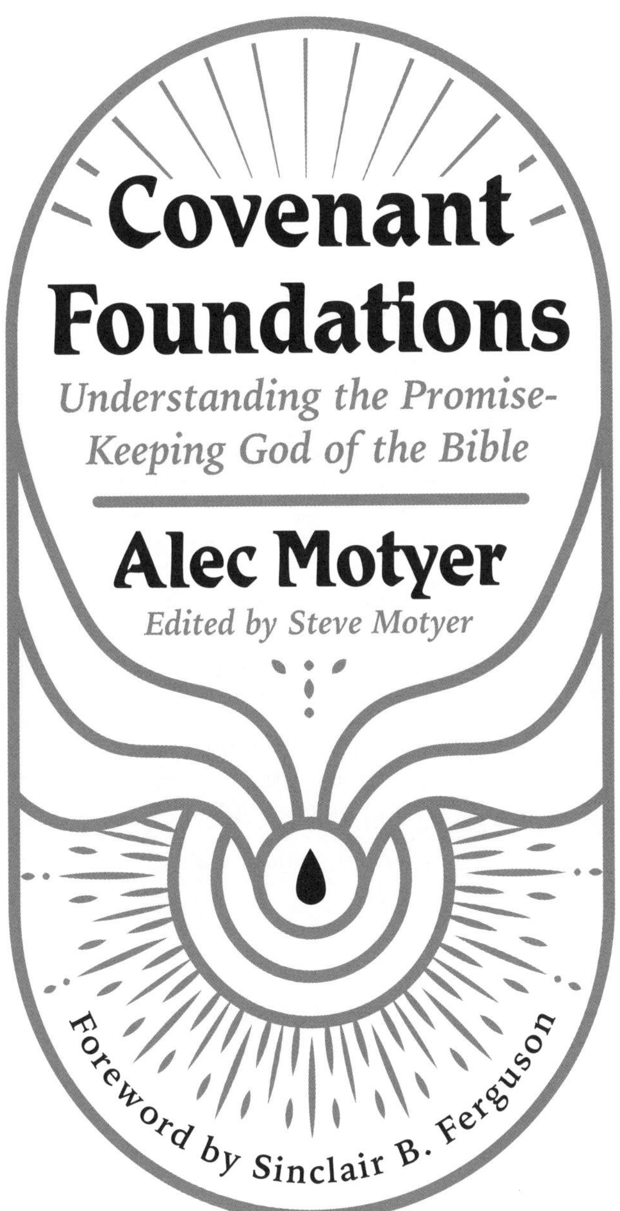

Covenant Foundations

Understanding the Promise-Keeping God of the Bible

Alec Motyer

Edited by Steve Motyer

Foreword by Sinclair B. Ferguson

CHRISTIAN FOCUS

paperback ISBN 978-1-5271-1100-4
ebook ISBN 978-1-5271-1144-8

10 9 8 7 6 5 4 3 2 1

Published in 2024
by
Christian Focus Publications Ltd,
Geanies House, Fearn, Ross-shire,
IV20 1TW, Great Britain.

www.christianfocus.com

Cover design by
Catriona Mackenzie

Printed and bound by
Bell & Bain, Glasgow

Contents

Foreword

Alec Motyer – A Personal Appreciation

It is a privilege to introduce this little book – not only to underline the inherent value of these pages but also to express a few words of personal appreciation for its author, Dr Alec Motyer, and to try to say about him what many of us who admired him were never able to say to him.

I first heard the name Alec Motyer when I was still in my teens, I had gone to St George's-Tron Church in the centre of Glasgow to listen to a 'landline' broadcast from the Keswick Convention. Re-imagining the scene now almost requires an exercise in time travel! For this early 1960s version of a live web stream involved a group of people sitting in silence in a Glasgow church listening to disembodied voices from a massive tent pitched 140 miles away in the English Lake District. For all practical purposes it was a group-listen to a publicly broadcasted telephone call!

In those days, echoes of the original pattern of 'The Keswick Message' could still be heard, although the message itself had gone through a process of considerable transformation (no doubt in part due to the influence of men like Alec Motyer). A 'Bible Reading' or consecutive exposition of a book or series of chapters occupied the mornings. During the rest of the day several half-hour-length sermons were preached on the theme of the day, moving systematically from sin to forgiveness to the ministry of the Spirit and then spiritual 'fulness' and service. In the evening gatherings two messages were preached with the singing of a hymn in between. All of the speakers sat together on the platform behind the preacher, like so many Aarons and Hurs holding up the hands of Moses. By the 1960s their experience was slightly less nerve-racking than it must have been in the Convention's earlier days when such was the emphasis on the Spirit's ministry that it was said only the chairman knew which of the speakers would be invited to preach on any given evening!

On that, to me never-to-be-forgotten evening, Alec Motyer was introduced as one of the preachers. If memory serves he expounded the closing section of Galatians 6. It was a model of Christ-honouring, cross-centred, expository ministry.

The New England pastor-theologian Jonathan Edwards once wrote that the critical issue in preaching is the impression made on the hearers *at the time* and suggested that any after-effects are likely to be related to that impression. As though a confirmation of that principle, I date from that exposition my first sense of the spiritual force of Paul's words 'I bear on my body the marks of Jesus' (Gal. 6:17). I suspect I have never thought about them without remembering that July evening.

Over the following years, as this sermon remained in my memory banks, and I encountered Alec Motyer's many books, and had fragmentary contact with him, I realized that my teenage assessment of the value of his ministry had been, if anything, an undervaluation. For now, I discovered that coupled with his scholar's learning and his evident love for the Scriptures and for those to whom he expounded them, was a rapier-like wit, and an endearing desire to encourage the next generation of ministers. An irresistible combination.

Thankfully for us all, these features are embedded in his books – including expositions of (at least) Exodus, Deuteronomy, the Psalms, Isaiah (two different commentaries and a devotional guide!), Amos, Zephaniah and Haggai,

Philippians, 1 Thessalonians, and James, as well as outstandingly helpful guides to Old Testament Theology and preaching. It is a testimony to his work that two friends who have been among the most listened-to preachers in my lifetime, the late Tim Keller of Redeemer Church in New York, and Alistair Begg of Parkside Church in Cleveland – men in very different situations, and with differing preaching styles (as it should be), felt a common debt to his works. Indeed, Tim once commented that 'my young self was thunderstruck' the first time he heard Alec Motyer speak.

But these would simply be the better-known names in a long litany of ministers and preachers who would gladly acknowledge how much they have benefitted from his ministry and in some cases to his personal friendship. Many of us certainly owe him a debt of which he almost certainly knew little or nothing. When he entitled his study of Old Testament biblical theology, *Look to the Rock*, he was referring to the Lord God. But Alec Motyer himself was also something of a lighthouse rock. With one or two other men of similar stature he stood out in his generation and did so without the vast volume of evangelical scholarship to which we have access today. His genius lay in his appreciation of the sheer livingness of Scripture not merely as a document to be analysed for purposes of scholarship but as the word and words of the living God to his people. He thus stood in the great tradition of men who were spiritually minded biblical scholars, and standing on their shoulders helped us to see a little further.

I first encountered this material in a photocopied transcription of lectures Alec Motyer gave at the annual conference of the Theological Students Fellowship[1] over the New Year period of December 1972 and January 1973.

1. The sub-section for theology students of what was then Inter-Varsity Fellowship (IVF), now The Universities and Colleges Christian Fellowship (UCCF).

How they came into my hands is now, like Nebuchadnezzar's dream, hidden from me! But here, to my surprise, was an *Irish Anglican* underscoring the biblical theme of the covenant that had once been front and centre in *Scottish Presbyterian* theology but had largely fallen on tough times.

Thus, Alec Motyer had become a kind of modern equivalent of the 17th century Irish Archbishop of Armagh, James Ussher (also Dublin-born and Trinity College Dublin educated) who had put Scottish Presbyterians like me in his debt by the influence the covenant theology of his *Irish Articles of Religion* had on the composition of our *Confession of Faith*! Here, albeit in modest photocopied form, was a fresh injection of covenant-centred, biblical theology. On the south side of the Scottish Border appreciation of the centrality of covenant theology had long absented itself; and on the north side by the time of the mid-19th century one of the country's great theologians, Hugh Martin, was lamenting its demise. Thankfully now expositions of biblical teaching on God's covenants can readily be found. But in many ways these lectures were like the cloud the size of a man's hand Elijah's servant saw – the harbinger of what was yet to come.

So, the discovery of the transcriptions was both a surprise and a joy. Looking back now I wish a publisher in the early 1970s had urged Alec Motyer himself to work the material into something like this book. For the original lectures provided in brief compass is a readily accessible, rich, and clear exposition of a biblical theme that belongs to spine of the Bible story, gives coherence to our understanding of its message, helps us better to know Christ, and puts marrow into our spiritual bones. But now, through the good offices of Dr Steve Motyer, the wish is a reality. He has not only been willing to allow the publication of his father's lectures but has also given his own time and energy to editing and formatting the raw materials of the original transcriptions with an understanding and sensitivity only a son could have. Do not miss his own reflections in his Postscript!

I met Alec Motyer only once, although we had some contact thereafter. He was everything I might have hoped: welcoming to a much younger man, easy to talk to, with a well-honed sense of humour and a generous spirit of encouragement and ongoing interest. He was not impressed with himself, and he knew not to be impressed by externals. He loved the church of Christ and the people of God. All that was obvious. He seemed to me to be the same in personal form as he was in book form – which is always both a relief and a delight to find whenever you meet people you have admired from afar through their writings.

The last report I heard of Alec Motyer the preacher came from one of our sons. He had come, along with his friend the late Richard Bewes (formerly rector of All Souls Church in London), to speak at the mid-week meeting of his congregation in Inverness in the Scottish Highlands. Our son's first reaction on seeing him was a sinking feeling that he had invited such a frail-looking elderly gentleman to preach! But when the time came, it was as if new life had been breathed into him – so energized was he by his love for the word of God and the people of God. No wonder then that Alec Motyer's name is still honoured, and that many of us are ongoingly grateful for the influence of his life and ministry, for his friendly encouragement, and for the inheritance he has left to us in his books.

Fifty years ago, the lectures on *Covenant Theology in the Old Testament* seemed to me to be just what was needed – a clear, concise, biblical account of the covenants of God and the God of the covenants. It still is. And so, thankfully, with *Covenant Foundations: Understanding the Promise-Keeping God of the Bible* now in our hands we can say of

Alec Motyer what was said of a figure from the early pages of the Hebrew Bible he loved so much: 'through his faith, though he died, he still speaks' (Heb. 11:4). And thanks to Christian Focus Publications and Steve Motyer, a new generation of readers can continue to hear his voice.

Sinclair B Ferguson
November 2023

Old Testament Covenant Theology

Why have you picked up a book on 'Covenant Theology'? You must already have some idea that this is a great theme to study and think about, in spite of the off-putting title! Let's face it, both 'covenant' and 'theology' are not words on everyone's lips. You don't hear them at the supermarket checkout or the school gate. 'Covenant' feels like a lawyer's word, technical and abstruse. 'Theology' feels intellectual and distant from everyday life, and the cause of some bitter arguing. But do you already think that there might be more to it than this? You're right to think so.

Let me let you into a secret: these words will change your feelings about God, and about your relationship with God, and will give you new confidence about your faith, your family and your future. That's worth having! Keep reading.

You see, 'covenant' is not a lawyer's plaything: it's a great biblical word, which takes us to heart of what God is doing in the world through our Lord Jesus Christ, who came as the fulfilment of what God had been doing through Israel. The whole Bible is held together by the word 'covenant'. At its heart, the biblical covenant is about God making and keeping promises to rescue us and establish us as His people.

And 'theology' simply describes what we do, when we study things like the biblical covenant, and put together the story of God's action, first in Israel and then in and through the Lord Jesus. 'Covenant theology', therefore, is just telling the story of God's action to make and keep His promises to save us, His people. If you're like me, you will want to be involved in that story. You won't want to miss out on anything that God is doing through His 'covenant'. You'll want in!

The Bible is a unity. We have it in two bits, of course, which we call the 'Old Testament' and the 'New Testament', and for us the second bit is especially important because that's where Jesus comes in. But for Jesus the Old Testament was simply 'the Scriptures,' the Word of God. And when we look at the Old Testament simply as 'God's Word', we realise that it prepares the way for Jesus, so that we can rightly understand Him. The foundations for the biblical covenant are all laid in the Old Testament, and first we need to understand it correctly there. Then we'll have our ducks in a row, so that we can rightly understand the New.

That's the purpose of this little book. We focus on the Old Testament, although we'll be glancing frequently across to the New. And here's a really fascinating fact: the covenant theme in the Bible really does begin at the beginning. We will spend most of our time in the 'books of Moses', the five books with which the Bible begins, often called 'the Pentateuch'. And within them, our focus will chiefly be on Genesis and Exodus, the first two. Of the seven chapters ahead of you, chapter one focuses on Genesis, and chapter two, on the first part of Exodus. Then in chapter three, we land up at Mount Sinai in the middle chapters of Exodus. Chapter four focuses on the last part of Exodus, and Leviticus. In chapter five we are chiefly in Leviticus and Deuteronomy, with a few little glances ahead to the prophets. Chapter six moves on to

Judges and the books of Samuel, and then in chapter seven we land up firmly in the prophets and look ahead to the New Testament. So you can see how absolutely foundation-laying the covenant is, for the message of the whole Bible.

I hope very much that you will enjoy this journey through the Scriptures with me. I have a goal, in writing this book. Will you add your own goal, in reading it? My goal is that together we can gain a clear biblical understanding of God's covenant love for us in Christ. Will you make it your goal, truly to grasp that covenant love for yourself and see yourself as part of God's great covenant story?

1

Covenant and Promise –Noah and Abraham

We begin our study of Old Testament Covenant Theology at the start of the Old Testament!—specifically, with the stories of Noah and Abraham in the book of Genesis. These stories mark the point at which the covenant theme begins to take shape, and give us clear indications of the *theology* involved in the idea of 'covenant'. In the case of both Noah and Abraham, we can see clearly how the covenant focuses upon *salvation*.

The 'covenant' idea in the Old Testament can be very simply summarised in the statement, 'God makes and keeps promises.' And if we press behind the idea and ask the great question 'Why does He do it?' we discover that, in making promises, God is moved simply by His own nature. Whatever the human circumstances to which He responds, the pressure God feels to make promises comes from His own heart. And then when it comes to *keeping* them, God acts in His own all-sufficient strength.

As we shall see in this book, the word 'all' in the expression 'all-sufficient' needs to be emphasised. God does not take anyone into partnership. He is not only totally able to keep His promises without assistance, but He insists upon doing so. Our first focus in this chapter is the story of Noah, where the idea of 'covenant' first appears, very dramatically and without any forewarning. Noah's story will teach us that *the God of the covenant reveals Himself as God the Saviour.* The point of God's promises is that He pledges Himself to a total work of *salvation*—the central theme of the covenant.

1. Noah.

The promise of salvation comes to Noah (Gen. 6–9) in relation to a very real and objective *threat.* Noah's whole world was under threat from God's wrath. A glance back at the chapters preceding Noah's story sets the scene for us: following the story of the fall in chapter 3, Genesis 4 and 5 are entirely given to showing the appalling spread of sin. In chapter 4 sin spreads to the descendants of Adam, and corruption increases. In chapter 5 we see sin's universal impact, for even though the men of that pre-flood generation lived to enormous ages, just one epitaph is written over each of them: 'and he died.'[1] However they managed to prolong their days, the power of sin and death prevailed and 'reigned' over them, as Paul puts it in Romans 5:14.

Genesis 6 then begins with a mysterious story which seems to mark a line across history for God. The action of the 'sons of God' in seizing 'the daughters of men' leads God to say, 'My spirit shall not abide (or 'strive'[2]) with humans forever' (6:1-3 NIV). God's determined 'No!' is then unpacked in detail:

1. See verses 5, 8, 11, 14, 17, 20, 27, 31.

2. It is not clear what this Hebrew verb really means. Either translation is possible.

> The LORD saw that the wickedness of man was great in the earth, and that every intention of the thoughts of his heart was only evil continually. And the LORD regretted that he had made man on the earth, and it grieved him to his heart. So the LORD said, 'I will blot out man whom I have created from the face of the land, man and animals and creeping things and birds of the heavens, for I am sorry that I have made them. (Gen. 6:5-7)

Notice how the word 'man' rings out repeatedly in this narrative. Verse 5 gives us the divine *assessment* (God sees human wickedness). Verse 6 tells us the divine *reaction* (God regrets creating human beings). Then verse 7 summarises the divine *resolve:* He determines to destroy the human race. And Noah belongs right in there! The story does not explain that God determines to destroy every human being except Noah. He starts with the rest of the world, under God's 'wrath', facing the objective threat of divine judgment, a corrupt man in a corrupt world heading for destruction.

But the covenant God is a Saviour. When humans are under threat of destruction—even by Him!—something impels Him to rescue them. That's what the story of Noah is all about. Let's lift this truth out of the narrative and explore three aspects of this divine impulse to act in response to human corruption, as they emerge in this story:

(1) The judgment of God.

There is no need to say much more under this heading. God is the sole sovereign in His own world. He does not have to ask permission to pass judgment. When He sees a situation requiring a universal judgment (as here), He says 'I will destroy.' But into this determination to judge there comes—

(2) The mercy of God.

After God's declaration of the coming destruction of humankind and of all other living creatures (Gen. 6:7) comes the simple comment, 'But Noah found favour in the eyes of the LORD' (6:8). Older translations have 'grace' here, rather than 'favour', and the expression that someone 'found grace' in another's eyes occurs frequently in the Old Testament (some twenty-seven times, in fact). We meet it, for instance, later in Genesis with Lot and the angels (Gen. 19:19), and with Joseph before Potiphar (29:4)—and elsewhere in the Old Testament with Moses before the Lord (Exod. 33:12), with Gideon before the angel (Judges 6:17), and with Ruth before Boaz (Ruth 2:10). We must notice something vital about this phrase: wherever it occurs, it points to the *meritlessness* of the one 'receiving' the grace. In fact, we could well focus its meaning simply by understanding it backwards: 'grace found Lot / Moses / Gideon / Ruth / Noah'—grace reaches out and lights on an unworthy object. The scriptural understanding of 'Noah found grace' is indeed that 'grace found Noah': into his meritless situation, under God's wrath and impending judgment, came the unmerited grace of God.

It is really important to notice how Genesis safeguards this truth against misunderstanding. The next verse (6:9) introduces Noah as 'a righteous man, blameless in his generation' who 'walked with God.' Some, of course, have suggested that we should read these verses the other way round—arguing that verse 9 supplies the *reason* for verse 8, that Noah 'finds grace' before the Lord *because of* his righteousness. But verse 9 begins with a new heading, in fact with one of Genesis' own chapter headings: 'These are the generations of Noah.' The introductory phrase 'These are the generations of

…' occurs some twelve times in Genesis, and makes a very interesting study in its own right. It always has the effect of drawing a line across the narrative and focusing our attention on a new phase or element of the story.[3]

So we are not invited—in fact we are not even permitted by Genesis—to reverse the order of verses 8 and 9. This would not only ignore the significance of Genesis' own chapter heading, which marks a new start in verse 9, but it would also put Genesis out of line with the rest of Scripture. Scripture forbids the thought that God rewards us for our goodness when He chooses us and shows us 'grace'. Verse 9 does not tell us *why* Noah was chosen, but shows us the evidence *that* he was chosen. Noah displays the *marks* of the truly elect, the marks of the man or woman upon whom mercy has come from God. Noah found grace; grace found Noah—and transformed him.

This man, found by grace, is the first to hear God speak the word 'covenant' in the Bible:

> I will bring a flood of waters upon the earth to destroy all flesh in which is the breath of life under heaven. Everything that is on earth shall die. But I will establish my covenant with you, and you shall come into the ark … (Gen. 6:17-18)

'My covenant' is shorthand for 'my promise of salvation'. Like all other human beings, Noah is death-bound, destined to 'perish': but into this deadly situation comes the covenant, expressed in the provision of the ark. And the word 'establish' is important—frequently used in connection with the covenant in the Old Testament. It is a vivid word, literally 'I will make the covenant

---

3. See e.g. Gen. 2:4, 5:1 (Adam), 10:1 (Noah's sons), 11:27 (Terah), 25:12 (Ishmael)—etc.

stand up': as though the covenant was inoperative or in suspense, and God is bringing it to life, making it leap to its feet. So its inner meaning is 'I will set my covenant in operation, I will make it take action—and you will enter the ark!' If on the one hand the wrath of God is flooding in, overwhelming a corrupt world, on the other hand the agency of the covenant is springing into action, laying hold of Noah in order to protect him while the world is perishing.

(3) The righteousness of God.

It is important to note that God is not denying His own nature as judge, by showing mercy. Noah still has to endure the flood. God doesn't say to him, 'My covenant is like a divine helicopter which is going to lower an escape harness and lift you up to heaven until I have finished with the earth.' The 'escape' was an ark, which wrapped him around and preserved him in the midst of the waters of judgment. He was so secured by the covenant, that the very form the judgment took guaranteed his salvation—because 'the ark floated on the face of the waters' as they rose (Gen. 7:18).

After all, it is no salvation—not even a pleasure!—to be locked up in an ark for nearly ten months.[4] It is like living in a zoo with your in-laws! There is nothing saving about the ark in itself. It was a single-use vessel, designed just for this one occasion, to keep Noah and his family safe. This covenant-making and covenant-keeping God is a God of the utmost righteousness who remains just. He is not dealing with Noah on the basis of favouritism or special action. He is acting in response to what sin deserves, and *yet* He sets Himself forth as the Saviour of sinners.

4. See Gen. 7:11, 8:13.

The covenant sign.

We must look briefly at this before we move on to Abraham. The story of Noah reaches its climax in Genesis 9 with God's promise to Noah, 'Behold, I establish my covenant with you and your offspring after you, and with every living creature that is with you' (Gen. 9:9-10). Specifically, this covenant promise is that 'never again shall all flesh be cut off by the waters of the flood' (9:11), and it is *actioned* by the giving of a sign:

> This is the sign of the covenant that I make between me and you and every living creature that is with you, for all future generations: I have set my bow in the cloud, and it shall be a sign of the covenant between me and the earth. When I bring clouds over the earth and the bow is seen in the clouds, I will remember my covenant that is between me and you and every living creature of all flesh. And the waters shall never again become a flood to destroy all flesh. Whenever the bow is in the clouds, I will see it and remember the everlasting covenant between God and every living creature of all flesh that is on the earth. (Gen. 9:12-16)

Covenant signs are given by the covenant God, to declare covenant promises to covenant people. They are tokens and guarantees of God's word. It is fascinating to notice that, in this case, the sign is not first and foremost a 'word' to Noah at all. Rather, God gives it as a reminder *for Himself:* 'When the bow is in the clouds, *I will see it and remember* the everlasting covenant' (9:16). God lets Noah—and us—into the secret: He tells us what the rainbow means to Him, so that the sign of the covenant begins to speak to us, too, assuring us of God's commitment. The sign reminds first God, and then us, of the covenant promise He has made.

2. Abraham.

As in the Noah narrative, we discover that God is the *sole agent* in Abraham's story, in making and implementing His covenant promises. This is sometimes called 'monergism', a technical theological term that underlines the thought that we cannot contribute anything to our salvation, but God does everything. In fact, nothing else is tolerable or possible.

This appears especially through the focus on Abraham's childlessness. His story begins with the childless state of his marriage to Sarah (Gen. 15:2: 'I continue childless …'), but it then focuses on how God specifically *disallows* any contribution from Abraham to solve the problem. It was possible, according to the law of the time, for Abraham to take a second wife and to have a child who would be recognised as Sarah's. And, prompted by Sarah herself, this is what Abraham does, having Ishmael by Hagar (the story is in Genesis 16). But God firmly disallows this as a contribution to the fulfilment of His promises. He leaves Abraham to cool his heels for thirteen further years—and then steps in and takes His own action to enable Sarah to have a child. The narrative is very careful to tell us that this happens totally by God's enabling.[5] God's promises are fulfilled by God's means at God's time—full stop!

So a simple story of a childless marriage turns into a wonderful demonstration of how God keeps His promises. Isaac was born by the normal processes of human reproduction, but both the initiative and the outcome were totally God's. The book of Genesis is like so much of the rest of Scripture: as Leon Morris says of John's Gospel, it is 'a pool in which a child may wade,

5. See Gen. 17:17–18:15, 21:1-7.

and an elephant can swim.'[6] Many of us have loved and revelled in the stories of Genesis from early childhood, but the more we read them, the deeper we realise they are. Profound biblical theology emerges from a simple story about a childless couple to whom children were promised.

The stories of Noah and Abraham hold the same message, in relation to a different threat. In Noah's case the threat is external, from God's wrath. In Abraham's case the threat is internal, from his and Sarah's inability to have children. But both Noah and Abraham were in no position to 'co-operate' in their own rescue. They both had to take action, but the initiative and the outcome were God's, and His alone. All Noah and Abraham can do is take the servant's place, submit to God's will and do what He tells them. As we have just seen, the story of Abraham in particular disallows the whole notion of human co-operation with God in the fulfilment of the divine promises. The covenant points to a salvation which is *all of God,* both in dealing with our 'internal' factors and in safeguarding us objectively, as His elect, from His own wrath.

The story of Abraham displays God's action in at least three ways:

(1) God chooses: His work of election.

There is a pivotal moment in Abraham's story, described in Genesis 15:6: 'He believed the LORD, and he counted it to him as righteousness.' Faced with his childlessness, Abraham chooses to believe God's promise that his offspring will be as numerous as the stars in the sky (Gen. 15:5). When Paul unpacks this story in Romans 4, he finds here the glorious doctrine of 'justification

---

6. Leon Morris, *The Gospel According to John* (New International Commentary; Grand Rapids: Wm B. Eerdmans Publishing Co., 1971), p. 7.

by faith', and underlines that Abraham simply took his stand on the promises of God:

> He did not weaken in faith when he considered his own body, which was as good as dead (since he was about a hundred years old), or when he considered the barrenness of Sarah's womb. No distrust made him waver concerning the promise of God, but he grew strong in his faith ... (Rom. 4:19-20)

His human situation was totally hopeless, but Abraham simply believed in *God's* outcome. A tremendous moment in his story! But in case Abraham should think that in any way he was being rewarded for his faith, God immediately reminds him of where his story began:

> I am the LORD, who brought you out from Ur of the Chaldeans to give you this land to possess. (Gen. 15:7)

Behind Abraham's story lie the choice, the impulse and the movement of God alone. Paul makes precisely this point in Romans 4.[7] Scripture simply insists on the priority and primacy of God's work in Abraham's life. Because God is at work in him, Abraham has come to this moment of total human failure and inability—and so also to this moment of faith.

(2) God commits: His work of self-obligation.

The story continues in Genesis 15 with Abraham's question, 'O Lord GOD, how am I to know that I shall possess it [the promised land]?'[8] How can Abraham be sure that God will keep His promise? The incident that follows gives us the answer. God tells Abraham to set up a very elaborate sacrificial arrangement. He has to take a variety of animals, great and small, to kill them and arrange their carcasses so as to leave a pathway

7. See Rom. 4:3-5.

8. Gen. 15:8.

between the slaughtered bodies of the animals. There are two vital things to notice about this strange story:

(a) These sacrifices are set up for God's sake. Literally translated, God's command begins 'Take *for me* ...' (Gen. 15:9), and then the next verse repeats the words 'for me' in describing Abraham's response. He did precisely what he was told, aware that this action is not for him but for God. Sacrifice is not a technique whereby human beings can twist God's arm. It is a provision that *God* makes for Himself.

(b) In line with this, *God is the sole agent* in the ceremony which centres upon these slaughtered animals. Just as Adam was anaesthetised when God took a rib to form Eve,[9] so now God applies a divine anaesthetic and puts Abraham out of action, so that he can be no more than an observer. He is immobilised while God acts alone:

> When the sun had gone down and it was dark, behold, a smoking firepot and a flaming torch passed between these pieces. On that day the LORD made a covenant with Abram. (Gen. 15:17-18)

We learn from Jeremiah what this 'passing between the pieces' meant: it signified taking a powerful and terrible oath,[10] illustrated also in 1 Samuel 11 when Saul sent the severed pieces of two oxen around the tribes of Israel in order to summon them to battle. The pieces carried a curse: 'This is what will be done to the oxen of anyone who does not immediately down tools and follow Saul!' (1 Sam. 11:7).

In Genesis 15 God takes this total covenant obligation upon Himself, because Abraham is made to sleep and so is disallowed from passing through the sacrifice

9. Gen. 2:21.

10. See Jer. 34:18.

that enacts the covenant between him and God. God is saying, 'If this covenant is broken, I will take the covenant curse upon myself.' Genesis doesn't pause at this point to spell out the implications, but in the light of the rest of Scripture we can see Calvary coming, the day when God in Christ became a curse for us.[11] This work of *self-obligation* on God's part is a truly remarkable feature of Abraham's story.

(3) God transforms: His work of regeneration.
The third stress in Genesis' account of God's covenant with Abraham appears in chapter 17. Thirteen long years have passed since the dramatic promise and sacrificial enactment of the covenant in chapter 15. Ishmael has been born, but no other children. Abraham is now ninety-nine. Suddenly God appears to Him and breaks his silence:

> 'I am God Almighty; walk before me and be blameless, that I may make my covenant between me and you, and may multiply you greatly.' Then Abram fell on his face. And God said to him, 'Behold, my covenant is with you, and you shall be the father of a multitude of nations.' (Gen. 17:1-4)

And before Abraham can react to this extraordinary re-affirmation of the promise, God underlines it:

> 'No longer shall your name be called Abram, but your name shall be Abraham, for I have made you the father of a multitude of nations.' (Gen. 17:5)

God comes in regenerating power to make the man into a new man, symbolised by the change of his name[12]—to

---

11. See Gal. 3:13.

12. The point is not what Abram's old and new names mean, but simply the fact that his name—and thus his whole person—is being transformed by God. In fact his old name (Abram) meant 'exalted father' (a name which must have constantly reminded him of God's promise, through those long

give him capacities which he did not have before. He makes the childless man a father on a colossal scale. And then God wraps up this promise in a new covenant sign, the sign of circumcision.

Genesis 17:1-14 falls into two parts, which both focus on the word 'covenant'. In part one (vv. 1-8), the covenant is defined in a series of *promises:*

- First, *personal:* 'My covenant is with *you*, and *you* shall be the father of a multitude of nations' (v. 4). In line with this focus on Abraham personally, God gives him a new name.
- Second, *domestic:* the nature of Abraham's amazing future family is declared, 'I will make you exceedingly fruitful, and I will make you into nations' (v. 6).
- Third, *spiritual:* 'I will establish my covenant between me and you and your offspring after you throughout their generations for an everlasting covenant, to be your God to you and to your offspring after you' (v. 7). God pledges Himself to live in a spiritual relationship with Abraham and his descendants as their God.
- Fourth, *territorial:* 'I will give to you and to your offspring after you the land of your sojournings, all the land of Canaan, for an everlasting possession' (v. 8).

And finally the promises are all wrapped up in the central and most important feature of the covenant promise, 'and I will be their God' (v. 8). Following the dramatic sacrifices in chapter 15, we know that these

---

years of childlessness), and his new name (Abraham) sounds in Hebrew like 'father of many'.

promises are not passing thoughts but deeply serious oaths to which God binds Himself.

Then in part two (vv. 9-14) the covenant appears in a different way:

> And God said to Abraham, 'As for you, you shall keep my covenant, you and your offspring after you throughout their generations. This is my covenant, which you shall keep, between me and you and your offspring after you: Every male among you shall be circumcised.' (vv. 9-10)

The covenant was a series of promises in verses 3-8, but now it is circumcision. This is because circumcision (literally) *incorporates* the promises as 'a sign of the covenant between me and you' (v. 11). It is the covenant's visible expression, just as the rainbow was for Noah. In both cases—the rainbow, and circumcision—something visible declares God's promises and the status of the recipient of the promises. So every time Abraham (not Abram!) saw the mark of circumcision in his body he could declare 'That means me! I am the man to whom God has made promises. God has gone on oath to me!' Covenant signs declare covenant promises to covenant people.

3. Noah and Abraham together.

We round off this chapter by asking, 'What did it mean for Noah and Abraham, to be covenant people receiving covenant promises?' In a nutshell, it meant three things: that they were (a) chosen, (b) for a purpose, and therefore (c) placed under an obligation. It meant *election, purpose and law:*

(1) Election.

Noah and Abraham were both what they were because God *chose* them to be so. Their stories start with God's election of them. Noah was immersed in the world's corruption until grace found him (Gen. 6:8). Abraham was stuck in Ur of the Chaldeans until God brought him out (Gen. 15:7). In both cases—especially visible in Noah's case—God's *mercy* lay behind God's choice. God was fulfilling His own purpose, and so 'grace found Noah'.

(2) Purpose.

Both Noah and Abraham were chosen by God for the sake of others, to mediate God's blessing beyond themselves. The covenant God establishes with Noah is 'with you and your offspring after you, and with every living creature that is with you ... every beast of the earth.'[13] Several times the story underlines that Noah's family and the animals were 'with' Noah in the ark. They were not there in their own right, but because they were 'with' the covenant man. They came under the benefit of the covenant God had made with Noah.[14]

Similarly God's call to Abraham (then Abram, of course) begins with a dramatic promise of universal blessing which must have seemed bizarre and deeply unsettling to Abram, then living quietly with his father Terah in Harran:

> Now the LORD said to Abram, 'Go from your country and your kindred and your father's house to the land that I will show you. I will make of you a great nation, and I will bless you and make your name great, so that you will be a blessing. I will bless those who bless you, and him who dishonours you I will curse, and in you all the families of the earth shall be blessed.' (Gen. 12:1-3)

13. Gen. 9:9-10; see also 9:12, 15, 16, 17.

14. See Gen. 6:18-20, 7:23, 8:1.

We cannot properly grasp this promise of universal blessing without looking back at the way in which Genesis paves the way for it, in chapter 11. The story of Babel (Gen. 11:1-9) gives us the third great act of divine judgment in Genesis 1-11, following on from the expulsion from the Garden and the Flood. But in this case, there is no story of mercy woven into the judgment, as there is with Adam and with Noah. Babel is judgment without mercy, it seems, as God comes down to inspect the city and the tower by which human beings are trying to 'make a name for ourselves, lest we be dispersed over the face of the whole earth' (11:4).

This attempt to save themselves is met by the divine negative with which God counters all such efforts, throughout the Bible: 'Oh No you won't!'—and God then imposes what they were trying to avoid, scattering human beings across the earth in confusion and division.

Is there no mercy in this act of judgment? Genesis seems immediately to change the subject, by taking us right back to Noah:

> These are the generations of Shem. When Shem was 100 years old, he fathered Arphaxad two years after the flood... (Gen. 11:10)

—and there follows a list of eight otherwise completely unknown patriarchs, whose lives left no ripple on the surface of history except that their names are included here. But God knew them and traced their line, until at last into this confused, post-Babel world a man named Terah was born,[15] whose son Abram will receive that enormous promise from God, 'all peoples on earth will be blessed through you.' God's purpose of mercy is still gloriously at work, addressing the judgment of Babel. Because of Babel, there are now 'peoples' scattered

15. See Gen. 11:24-27.

across the earth, and Abraham will mediate God's mercy to the entire world.

(3) Law.

As soon as Noah stepped out of the ark, God declared His law to him: 'God blessed Noah and his sons and said to them, "Be fruitful and multiply and fill the earth."'[16] They have a God-given calling to fulfil. And then God specifies how this must be accomplished, giving Noah laws concerning food and the sacredness of human life: 'You shall not eat flesh with its life, that is, its blood ... whoever sheds the blood of man, by man shall his blood be shed.'[17] Living under covenant promise means living under covenant law.

We see the same with Abraham, especially at the moment of his circumcision. In Noah's case, the covenant sign was entirely God's action. God hung up His warrior bow in the clouds to signify that the enmity was over between Him and all animate life. But in Abraham's case, God passed the action over to the covenant recipient. God did not become a divine surgeon and perform the circumcision Himself. Abraham had to do it, and his obedient action constituted the covenant at that very moment. The one action of circumcision brings together the promise and the obedient response to it—the two cannot be separated. So Abraham cannot look at the mark of circumcision and glory in the promises without also, at the same moment, being reminded of his commitment to obey God—to 'walk before me and be blameless' (Gen. 17:1).

So the law of God is written into the heart of the covenant idea. In our next chapter we will see how this theme develops as the story of the covenant moves on

16. Gen. 9:1.

17. Gen. 9:4, 6.

into Exodus and we meet the next great figure in the story, Moses.

2

The Normative Covenant –Moses and the Passover

The covenant story continues into Exodus. In fact we can draw a straight line from Noah and Abraham through to Moses, the Passover, the exodus from Egypt and the giving of the law at Sinai. This is the storyline introduced for us at the beginning of Exodus, where the covenant is made the key to the action about to unfold:

> During those many days the king of Egypt died, and the people of Israel groaned because of their slavery and cried out for help. Their cry for rescue from slavery came up to God. And God heard their groaning, and God remembered his covenant with Abraham, with Isaac, and with Jacob. God saw the people of Israel—and God knew. (Exod. 2:23-25)

Recall the circumstances here. At this point the people are not just slaves in Egypt, but also the focus of a genocidal plan put into action by Pharaoh.[1] And genocide would have been the outcome, except that *God remembered His covenant* (2:24)—and Exodus tells us how the covenant meant rescue and new life for Israel.

Initially Moses met huge setbacks when he came back to Egypt with the news of God's rescue plan. Far

1. See Exod. 1:15-22.

from agreeing to let Israel go, Pharaoh greatly increased his demands, and as a result Moses was rejected by the leaders of Israel themselves.[2] An enormous discouragement, right at the start of the story. But Moses knows how to deal with discouragement: he 'turned to the LORD' (5:22) with his complaint that, in spite of His promise, 'you have not delivered your people at all' (5:23).

God responds by reaffirming His promise and renewing Moses' vision. His words begin with a glorious 'now' (6:1): right at the moment of discouragement, God will step in to save Israel, because of His covenant:

> But the LORD said to Moses, 'Now you shall see what I will do to Pharaoh; for with a strong hand he will send them out, and with a strong hand he will drive them out of his land.' God spoke to Moses and said to him, 'I am the LORD. I appeared to Abraham, to Isaac, and to Jacob, as God Almighty, but by my name the LORD I did not make myself known to them. I also established my covenant with them to give them the land of Canaan, the land in which they lived as sojourners. Moreover, I have heard the groaning of the people of Israel whom the Egyptians hold as slaves, and I have remembered my covenant. Say therefore to the people of Israel, "I am the LORD, and I will bring you out from under the burdens of the Egyptians, and I will deliver you from slavery to them, and I will redeem you with an outstretched arm and with great acts of judgement. I will take you to be my people, and I will be your God, and you shall know that I am the LORD your God, who has brought you out from under the burdens of the Egyptians. I will bring you into the land that I swore to give to Abraham, to Isaac, and to

2. See the story in Exod. 5.

> Jacob. I will give it to you for a possession. I am the LORD."' (Exod. 6:1-8)

Clearly 'covenant' is a key theme here!—it is the motivation underlying God's promised rescue, as with Noah and Abraham, picking up the great covenant promise made to Abraham, that He would be God to Abraham and to his 'offspring' after him, and seal that relationship by giving the land and many other things besides.[3]

It is not just the appearance of the word 'covenant' which is significant. Even more significant is the setting of the story: Pharaoh's genocidal plot against Israel was a fundamental challenge to God's promise to Abraham. At the start, God's word was, 'I will bless those who bless you, and him who dishonours you I will curse.'[4] Pharaoh didn't know that he was setting himself up to challenge the covenant. And when His covenant is challenged, God rises to defend it. In doing so, God brings the covenant to its 'normative' expression.

We must pause on this word 'normative'. The Exodus covenant story picks up two covenant ideas which were present in the stories of Noah and Abraham, and gives them a full explanation and elaboration—their normative statement within Old Testament theology: the great themes of *sacrifice* and *law*.

Let's glance back to Noah and Abraham. God made and kept a glorious promise of rescue to Noah, wrapping him in the ark and bearing him to safety over the waters of judgment into the new world. But once he lands 'on the mountains of Ararat,' and he and his extraordinary passenger-list have left the ark,[5] Noah's first act is to

---

3. Gen. 17:7-8–compare vv. 7-8 here.
4. Gen. 12:3.
5. Gen. 8:4, 18-19.

build an altar and to offer burnt offerings. The narrative gives no explanation at this point, as to why this was an appropriate first action, or why God then responds as He does, with a promise never again to destroy the world in this way.[6] But clearly it's right for the covenant man, Noah, to offer sacrifice.

In a similar vague and undefined way, *law* then appears in the narrative. God sets before Noah a brief pattern of life for the covenant man and his society, the broad principles by which humankind is to live in concert with all the other inhabitants of the earth as humans begin to 'teem on the earth and multiply in it'.[7] But no details are given.

We have already seen how the same two themes appear in the Abraham narrative. The covenant relationship rests on sacrifice, as God puts Himself on oath by marching between the severed carcasses.[8] Like Noah, Abraham had already offered sacrifices 'to the LORD,'[9] and will do so again very significantly when commanded to sacrifice Isaac for whom a ram is substituted at the last second.[10] But no explanation is given, as to why sacrifice is required, or how it works.

Similarly we noticed how the covenant sign, circumcision, is turned into a requirement, an act to be performed obediently by the covenant man. Genesis 17, where the sign is given, starts significantly on a note of law:

---

6. Gen. 8:21-22.
7. Gen. 9:1-7.
8. Gen. 15:7-21.
9. See Gen. 12:8, 13:18.
10. Gen. 22:1-14.

> I am God Almighty; walk before me, and be blameless, that I may make my covenant between me and you, and may multiply you greatly. (Gen. 17:1-2)

As we saw, the covenant is then defined in a series of four promises which are parcelled up into the applicatory sign of circumcision. So law is brought into the heart of God's covenant dealings. At this stage it is vague and undefined, simply 'walk before me and be blameless'—although we can say for sure that no *moment* of life is exempt from 'walk before me' and no *action* of life is left out of 'be blameless'. There is much room for further explanation and detail, although we can see how these two themes, sacrifice and law, begin to come into clearer focus as Noah's story leads into Abraham's.

The stage is set for Exodus! As we move through the story of God's dealings with Moses and Israel in Egypt, and as we trace the events of the Passover and their journey through the wilderness to their rendezvous with God at Mount Sinai, two things happen: (1) Sacrifice takes its place at the heart of the covenant, and is *explained*; and (2) Law takes its place at the heart of the covenant, and is *elaborated*. The covenant reaches its 'normative' form.

In the rest of this chapter we will focus on the first half of this covenant story, noticing how it begins with God's revelation of Himself to Moses, to Israel and to Pharaoh, and then how it continues with God's great actions in the plagues, in the Passover, and in the exodus itself. The way in which the story begins with God's self-revelation, so clear in Exodus 6:1-8 quoted above, is vital not just in Exodus but for biblical theology altogether. Let's look at this first.

1. The revelation of God in word and deed.

The order of the words here, 'word and deed', is deliberate and very important! It used to be fashionable among theologians to suggest that the task of theology is to reflect on God's actions and to draw the truth out of them—to look at what God does, and then to think (and teach) wisely and truly in response. Revelation thus takes place, it was held, in God's acts, not through words that God speaks. Old Testament theologian G. Ernest Wright famously summarised this view in his book *God Who Acts. Biblical Theology as Recital*: he argued that the Old Testament is simply concerned to *tell the story* of God's deeds—to bear witness to what He has done.[11] Archbishop William Temple expressed this view in his quip, 'There are no revealed truths; there are only truths of revelation.'[12] In other words, God does not commit Himself to propositional truths expressed in words which God Himself utters. Rather, all we have (both in the Bible, and in our own theology) is 'truths of revelation'—that is, truths which we will know if we manage to think correctly about God, as we reflect on what He has done. On this view Scripture is downgraded and becomes simply the first of a potentially never-ending line of attempts to interpret God and His actions in the world.

In response we can simply point out that this is not how it happens in Exodus 1-12! Here God's word of self-revelation *precedes* His saving actions. Revelation is not contained in a word which arises by *interpretation* of a deed: rather, revelation consists in a word which is subsequently *confirmed* by a deed. There is a snug

11. G.E. Wright, *God Who Acts. Biblical Theology as Recital* (Studies in Biblical Theology 8; SCM: London, 1952).

12. In William Temple, *Nature, Man and God* (Gifford lectures 1932–3 and 1933–4; Macmillan: London, 1934).

relationship between the two: first God commits Himself verbally to what He plans to do, and then confirms the truth of His words by doing precisely what He said. So Moses is not an interpreter after the event, but a man made wise before the event. We can unpick this by noticing several features of the story that illustrate this 'word and deed' relationship:

(a) God tells Moses that *everything He proposes to do arises from His commitment to 'the fathers'* (Exod. 3:6) and to the covenant (Exod. 6:5). Indeed, the narrator of the story makes precisely this point right at the start, so that we, the readers, are in no doubt (Exod. 2:24).

(b) The rescue of Israel begins with God's revelation of Himself, in the burning bush, as *a God of blazing holiness* (Exod. 3:5). This is the first time in the Bible that God's holiness is directly revealed in connection with His presence.

(c) God announces to Moses *His plan to bring His people out of Egypt:* 'I know their sufferings, and I have come down to deliver them' (Exod. 3:7-8).

(d) God *reveals Israel's special status* as God's 'firstborn son' (Exod. 4:22-23). God's rescue of Israel is based on this remarkable adoption of the nation, and Moses returns to Egypt armed with this awareness.

(e) God tells Moses *how events will actually play out.* His first task is to perform wonders showing God's authority—'See that you do before Pharaoh all the miracles that I have put in your power'. But Moses is also told that this strategy will not work: 'I will harden his heart, so that he will not let the people go.' The whole coming sequence of events is stated in outline before Moses goes back to Egypt: the initial signs simply provoke increasing opposition, and lead to a final showdown in which it is either God's first-born or Pharoah's.[13]

(f) Moses is made aware that God plans and *achieves redemption.* Nothing will stop Him. After his initial skirmish with Pharaoh, Moses hears God's purpose again:

> Say therefore to the people of Israel, 'I am the LORD, and I will bring you out from under the burdens of the Egyptians, and I will deliver you from slavery to them, and I will redeem you with an outstretched arm and with great acts of judgement.' (Exod. 6:6)

Here the word 'redeem' appears for the first time in the Bible in its full, normative sense.[14]

(g) These points all illustrate clearly how God reveals Himself and His plans before He acts. But more significant than all these is *the revelation of the meaning of His own name.* 'I am the LORD. I appeared to Abraham, to Isaac, and to Jacob, as God Almighty, but by my name the LORD I did not make myself known to them.'[15] God renews His commitment to the covenant by revealing His name as never before. This is so important that we must give more attention to it.

In many Bibles, when God is referred to as 'the LORD' using capital letters, the Hebrew actually has the divine name 'Yahweh'. The ESV quoted here follows this custom.[16] Some versions use 'Yahweh' directly (or 'Jehovah', another form of the same name).[17] The important point for us, thinking about this revelation of

---

13. See Exod. 4:21-23, where this whole scenario is laid out in a nutshell.

14. It occurs once before, in Gen. 48:16, but without its technical meaning within the covenant relationship.

15. Exod. 6:2-3.

16. So also e.g. TNIV, REB, CEV, NRSV.

17. For instance the Jerusalem Bible. The Moffatt version of the Bible translates 'Yahweh' with 'the Eternal', which gives entirely the wrong idea.

the name 'Yahweh' to Moses, is that it is closely related to the Hebrew verb 'to be'.[18] Strange to say, it is vital to grasp exactly what 'to be' means in Hebrew! Rather than some bare abstract idea of 'existence' in contrast to 'non-existence', in Hebrew 'being' means *living reality and active presence.* For instance, the frequent expression 'the word of the LORD came to …'[19] would literally be translated 'the word of the LORD *was* to …', expressing not motion but a lived, vital experience of the *presence* of God's word to the prophet. So by revealing Himself as 'Yahweh, the One Who Is' God is saying 'I am the God of living presence with my people.' And in this Exodus context, as God commits Himself to the covenant and to rescuing Israel, God's living presence means *action in relationship.* He takes Israel to be His adopted children, works redemption for them, overthrows the power of Pharaoh, and brings them out. He superintends the whole process, bringing it to the climax He has determined, and in particular ordaining the Passover with its shedding of blood at the heart of the events. Even the hardening of Pharaoh's heart is ascribed to the action of the same God who guarantees His living presence to His people.

Similarly, in the New Testament God further reveals His name to be 'the God and Father of our Lord Jesus Christ',[20] expressed pre-eminently in the work of Calvary and the resurrection, where 'in Christ God was reconciling the world to himself'.[21] As in Exodus, it is in

---

18. See Exod. 3:13-15, where this connection between 'Yahweh' (the LORD) and the verb 'to be' is particularly clear.

19. Very frequent in the prophets: for instance, some twenty times in Jeremiah, and forty-seven times in Ezekiel.

20. e.g. Col. 1:3.

21. 2 Cor. 5:19.

the *action* of redemption that God's nature (His name) is revealed.

This is very important when we consider the apparent contradiction between Genesis and Exodus over the name 'Yahweh'. In Exodus 6:3 God says that 'by my name Yahweh I did not make myself known' to Abraham, Isaac and Jacob. But these patriarchs clearly did know the name Yahweh: as we saw above, Abraham 'built an altar to the LORD' (i.e. Yahweh) in Bethel, 'and called upon the name of the LORD' (Gen. 12:8). Similarly Isaac 'prayed to the LORD' for his wife Rebekah to become pregnant (Gen. 25:21), and then later God reveals Himself to Jacob as 'the LORD, the God of Abraham your father and the God of Isaac' (Gen. 28:13).

What are we to make of this? Older scholarship built this apparent contradiction into an elaborate theory about different, conflicting sources underlying the Pentateuch (the five books of Moses). However, an awareness of 'being' in Hebrew as living, active presence helps us to understand it, and it turns out that the covenant is at the heart of the solution. Abraham, Isaac and Jacob knew the name Yahweh, but not its *meaning* as now revealed by this 'coming down' of God to meet His people's need and deliver them. This is now covenant in living action, never before seen. We discover what it really means is that God has committed Himself to be 'God to you and to your offspring after you' (Gen. 17:7): He will step in to 'redeem' them from slavery in Egypt, 'with an outstretched arm and with great acts of judgment' (Exod. 6:6), and will bring them into the land He promised to Abraham. And He now ties His very being, His name and nature as 'Yahweh', the One Who Is, to this vital, committed presence and redeeming action for His people in their need.[22] The patriarchs thought they knew Him, but not like this: not as the God of the Exodus now revealed to Moses and to Israel.

So now we will look more closely at God's action under our second heading.

2. The redemptive activity of God in confirmation of His word.

We have already touched on this in outline. Things happened in Egypt exactly as God said they would. Moses arrived before Pharaoh and started to perform the wonders God had commanded. Pharaoh reacted as predicted, with downright refusal. The plagues—nine of them—began to follow and, as foretold, effected no salvation. Pharaoh simply hardened his heart and increased the Israelites' bondage. Things worsened until Pharaoh broke off diplomatic negotiations with Moses: 'Get away from me; take care never to see my face again, for on the day you see my face you shall die.' Moses gives as good as he gets—'As you say! I will not see your face again' (Exod. 10:28-29). And the careful narrator of Exodus lets us know that, indeed, a turning-point has been reached:

> Moses and Aaron did all these wonders before Pharaoh, and the LORD hardened Pharaoh's heart, and he did not let the people of Israel go out of his land. (Exod. 11:10)

—as though to say to us, 'You see? It happened precisely as God said it would.' So the moment of climax has arrived. The stage has been set for the contest of the first-born, different from anything hitherto seen. Who

22. On this see further J.A. Motyer, *The Revelation of the Divine Name* (Tyndale Press: London, 1959).

will lose—Pharaoh's first-born, or the LORD's?[23] I think we know the answer. The outcome is certain, but the *setting* of the contest takes us by surprise. This final 'plague' is set within the long, detailed, and completely unexpected narrative of the Passover, in Exodus 12–13. The Israelites have to choose a lamb for each household and eat it 'in doors' in haste, ready to depart as soon as that terrible night is past, during which the first-born die in every house in Egypt. Why is this Passover meal given such prominence in the narrative?

To discover the reason for the Passover we need to ask another question first.

Why the plagues?

As we saw, God had told Moses in advance that the plagues would not work,[24] so why did God subject the Egyptians to this long drawn-out series of calamities? We already know that only the final contest of the first-born will 'bring home the bacon'—so why the blood, frogs, gnats, flies etc. The answer to this prepares the way for the Passover: the plagues show how God always mingles patience with judgment. He doesn't spring catastrophe on people. He approaches with quieter, less disastrous judgments, which serve as warnings and appeals. He gives people a chance to hear the cock crowing, to heed the warning and to turn to Him. In all He lets the cock crow nine times, so that when judgment finally comes it has been established beyond doubt that here is a people set in its opposition to God and unwilling to hear His word. God only brings in judgment when patience has been exhausted.

But when the final judgment, the contest of the first-born, arrives, it's clearly not just a matter of God

23. Remember Exod. 4:22-23.

24. See Exod. 4:21, 7:1-4.

simply rescuing His first-born, Israel, at the expense of all the first-born in Egypt. The Israelites have to prepare for this tenth and final plague with an elaborate ritual involving the selection and slaughter of a lamb for each household—a lamb which then has to be cooked and eaten in haste after its blood has been smeared around the door of the house.[25] The instructions go on to specify that this ritual must become an annual event—'you shall observe this day, throughout your generations, as a statute forever.'[26] But why?

Why the Passover?

The reason is clear. There were two nations in Egypt, and both of them—both the Egyptian captors and their Israelite captives—were resistant to the word of God. So when God comes in judgment *none* will escape, unless God has made some prior decision or commitment to guarantee the safety of some. And He has! As Israel's merciful, covenant-keeping God He has made promises to rescue His people, not just from bondage and slavery but also from the terrible consequences of His own wrath against sin. So He provides the Passover lamb and the smearing of its blood around the door, so that His people may shelter safely where the blood has been shed.

We saw the same thing with Noah.[27] With judgment looming, God wrapped Noah around with safety—the ark—so that when the blow fell, Noah and his family were saved in the midst of God's wrath. So now Israel is wrapped in the blood of the lamb, protected from the wrath and judgment that falls around them.

---

25. See Exod. 12:1-11.
26. Exod. 12:17.
27. See above, p x

Let's look more closely at the theology of this Passover event, the focus of God's action in keeping His promise to save His people. There are five key words which summarise the meaning of the Passover:

(a) Propitiation. To 'propitiate' means 'to appease wrath'—i.e. to take some action which will turn aside anger and its expression. And that is the setting of the Passover: it is an action, prescribed by God Himself, in response to God's wrathful judgment on Egypt:

> I will pass through the land of Egypt that night, and I will strike all the firstborn in the land of Egypt, both man and beast, and on all the gods of Egypt I will execute judgments: I am the LORD. (Exod. 12:12)

None of the gods of Egypt can propitiate this wrath—in fact, they fall under it too. Only one thing is able to do that:

> For the LORD will pass through to strike the Egyptians, and when he sees the blood on the lintel and on the two door-posts, the LORD will pass over the door and will not allow the destroyer to enter your houses to strike you. (Exod. 12:23)

Apart from the Passover blood, the destroyer would enter. And notice that the Israelites have to be inside their houses in order to be protected. Any Israelite wandering outside, having failed to heed these Passover instructions, would fall under the judgment. All alike were under God's wrath that night. The key verse makes this clear:

> The blood shall be a sign for you, on the houses where you are. And when I see the blood, I will pass over you, and no plague will befall you to destroy you, when I strike the land of Egypt. (Exod. 12:13)

Just being an Israelite does not save. Notice that God does not say 'When I see *you*' but 'when I see *the blood,* I will pass over you'. Putting it bluntly, there is something about the blood that changes God. When He sees it, He 'passes over' that house, and all inside are safe. Only the word 'propitiation' will do, to describe this. This is not about 'expiation', the theological word that describes the washing away of sin from our hearts. There is nothing here about the subjective state of God's people at this point, or about an inner experience of forgiveness. This is wholly about how God sees them, and how the Passover blood turns aside His wrath and 'propitiates' Him.

(b) Security (or *Salvation*). It is very clear that this story is not *just* about freeing Israel from suffering at the hands of their oppressors or from political bondage in Egypt. It *is* about this, but also about so much more: they need salvation—safety—not just from Egyptian whips but chiefly from the wrath of God and His determination to strike down the first-born throughout Egypt (see Exod. 12:29). And it is so simple: all they have to do is to:

> take a bunch of hyssop and dip it in the blood ... and touch the lintel and the two doorposts with the blood that is in the basin (12:22)

and then pass under that lintel into the house and stay there. Then they are safe. The blood on the door works in two directions: towards God, it means propitiation; towards the families of Israel gathered around the Passover meal inside the door, it means security.

(c) Substitution. Why is that blood so powerful?—sufficient to propitiate a wrathful God and provide security for His people? The narrative gives us clues to answer this question. We must notice that God's

judgment is about *death*. We must not allow modern sensitivities to blur the fact so clear in the narrative: God's judgment inflicts death on every family in Egypt—He comes in to *slay*, a terrible consequence of the repeated refusal to hear and obey His word:

> And Pharaoh rose up in the night, he and all his servants and all the Egyptians. And there was a great cry in Egypt, for there was not a house where someone was not dead. (Exod. 12:30)

A death in every house. But maybe here the narrator says more than he meant, for of course in Israelite houses the death was not of the first-born, but of the lamb. In those homes a death had taken place already, before the midnight visitation that brought such grief throughout the land, and such a change of heart towards the Israelites.[28]

We cannot resist the word 'substitution' to draw out the meaning here. The lamb dies, so that in Israelite houses protected by its blood there will be no other death. In fact the narrative rubs our noses in the equivalence between the lamb and the members of each household. They had to choose a lamb for each household, or for multiple households if families were small, and the principle of measurement was:

> according to the number of persons; according to what each can eat you shall make your count for the lamb. (Exod. 12:4)

To make sure the lamb matched exactly, they had to count both heads and stomachs! The lamb must be exactly right for the needs of God's people—and if they should over-estimate, then:

---

28. See Exod. 12:33-36.

> you shall let none of it remain until the morning; anything that remains until the morning you shall burn. (Exod. 12:10)

The lamb that died, under whose blood God's people sheltered, was matched exactly to their number and needs. That sounds like substitution! The mathematically inclined might object that only the first-born were at risk from God's judgment that night. But actually—as we have seen—the presupposition behind the whole Exodus narrative is that Israel, the nation, is God's first-born. This was to be Moses' very first message to Pharaoh: 'Thus says the LORD, "Israel is my firstborn son ... Let my son go that he may serve me."'[29] This is the son for whom the Passover lamb is the exact equivalent.

(d) Deliverance. The death of the lamb did not just make deliverance *possible* for God's people. It made it *actual,* and *inevitable.* Before the lamb died, they could not go. After the lamb died, they could not stay. They sprang out of Egypt like greyhounds from the gate, impelled by the Egyptians who were now desperate to get rid of them. This is why, elsewhere in the Old Testament, the focus is usually on what happens next, when Israel lands up trapped by the Red Sea, with the army of Egypt on one side and the sea on the other, and they hear Moses' great summons—a word addressed to all who have not yet entered fully into the Lord's deliverance—'Fear not, stand firm, and see the salvation of the LORD, which he will work for you today!'[30] The waters open before them, they pass through, the Egyptians attempt to follow and are drowned, and when the Israelites see the Egyptians dead on the shore they 'feared the LORD, and they believed in the LORD and

29. Exod. 4:22-23.

30. Exod. 14:13.

in his servant Moses.'[31] Then they knew for certain that they had truly been redeemed from the land of Egypt, and their bondage was over. Redemption accomplished and applied!

(e) Pilgrimage. This is the fifth word which floats up from the narrative, helping us to summarise the 'theology of Passover' we meet here. The Passover meal was a supper to be eaten as a breakfast, a quick bite with your coat on before rushing out of the house:

> In this manner you shall eat it: with your belt fastened, your sandals on your feet, and your staff in your hand. And you shall eat it in haste. It is the LORD's Passover. (Exod. 12:11)

Why the haste? Somehow the haste follows from it being 'the LORD's Passover.' Once they have eaten it, they can no longer live in Egypt. This meal is the first step on a journey. The people who walked in through the blood-stained door into security must immediately walk out again, into pilgrimage with their Saviour God. The Passover turns out to be the fulfilment of God's word to Abraham, 'Walk before me, and be blameless.'[32] Life with this God means *walking.* It doesn't mean hiding in the place of security, but being committed to pilgrimage—and this was signalled even as they ate the meal, already dressed for the road.

Now begins the long story of Israel's pilgrimage with her covenant God, as the redeemed stream out of Egypt into all that lies ahead. These five words—propitiation, security, substitution, deliverance and pilgrimage—have bubbled up for us out of the Passover story in Exodus. But they take us beyond Exodus. Travelling on, we

31. Exod. 14:31.

32. Gen. 17:1.

will find that they are at the heart of *Old Testament* covenant theology. And travelling further still—beyond the bounds of this little book—we discover that they are at the heart of *biblical* covenant theology, because, of course, Scripture speaks with one voice. The covenant God of the Old Testament is the covenant God of the New.

3

Covenant and Law –destination Sinai

In a good TV series each episode begins with a recap to remind us of the key moments so far, and to prepare us for the next steps. What have we seen so far in our exploration of Old Testament covenant theology?

- 'Covenant' is a key biblical word, from Noah onwards.
- It summarises God's binding commitment to stay in relationship with humankind and with Israel in particular, a commitment to save and rescue.
- We see the covenant in action through Moses when God 'comes down' to rescue Israel from Egypt ('redeem' is the biblical word).
- The provision of the Passover lamb and meal secured Israel's redemption from Egypt, and meant that they were committed to pilgrimage. They had no option but to go walking with their God.

Where is that walk taking them? First stop—Mount Sinai.

Two verses, from either side of Israel's time camped at the foot of Sinai, show how vital 'covenant' is to help us understand what happens there. First, hear God's very first words to His people when they arrive at the mountain:

> You yourselves have seen what I did to the Egyptians, and how I bore you on eagles' wings and brought you to myself. Now therefore, if you will indeed obey my voice and keep my covenant, you shall be my treasured possession among all peoples … (Exod. 19:4-5)

The covenant God addresses the covenant people in covenant terms. Then, after the sequence of events at Sinai, we read that Moses:

> took the Book of the Covenant and read it in the hearing of the people. And they said, 'All that the LORD has spoken we will do, and we will be obedient.' And Moses took the blood and threw it on the people and said, 'Behold the blood of the covenant that the LORD has made with you in accordance with all these words.' (Exod. 24:7-8)

The whole Sinai sequence of narratives is bracketed between these two assertions that Sinai is completely about God's *covenant* dealings with His people.

This is all rather surprising at first sight. We might have been inclined to think that Mount Sinai is just a staging-post *en route* to Israel's main destination, the promised land of Canaan. Yes, it's true that God is leading His people ultimately to Canaan in fulfilment of His promises. But we must not overlook the fact that Sinai was the primary destination towards which they were aiming when they left Egypt.

This emerges clearly in the course of the narrative. First, note God's promise to a very hesitant Moses in Exodus 3:12:

> I will be with you, and this shall be the sign for you, that I have sent you: when you have brought the people out of Egypt, you shall serve God on this mountain.

For Moses, the arrival at Mount Sinai, and the worship of God there, are the crown upon the whole exodus enterprise. When that happened, Moses would receive it as a divine token that God had engineered it all.

Secondly, in Exodus 3:18, when Moses is sent to open diplomatic negotiations with Pharaoh, these were the Lord's instructions:

> You and the elders of Israel shall go the king of Egypt and say to him, 'The LORD, the God of the Hebrews, has met with us; and now, please let us go a three days' journey into the wilderness, that we may sacrifice to the LORD our God.'

So their primary destination, on leaving Egypt, was this great planned sacrifice. Thirdly we should notice how the narrative lays great emphasis on the fact that God led Israel's journey through the wilderness. It starts with the simple statement that 'when Pharaoh let the people go ... God led them' (Exod. 13:17-18), and this is then elaborated as the story unfolds:

> The LORD went before them by day in a pillar of cloud to lead them along the way, and by night in a pillar of fire to give them light, that they might travel by day and by night. The pillar of cloud by day and the pillar of fire by night did not depart from before the people. (Exod. 13:21-22)

This was a journey under manifest divine leadership! It is vital to remember this as we notice what a tough journey the Israelites had, facing difficulty after difficulty on the road to Sinai. They were cornered between the sea and the pursuing Egyptian army—because God led them there.[1] They followed the pillars of cloud and fire for three days into the desert, and ran out of water.[2] Six weeks into the journey they ran out of food and faced starvation.[3] Then it was dying of thirst again, because God led them to Rephidim where 'there was no water for the people to drink.'[4] And then they had to fight off the Amalekites in the same place.[5] These huge challenges help us to read Exodus 13:17-18 with deeper understanding:

> When Pharaoh let the people go, God did not lead them by way of the land of the Philistines, although that was near. For God said, 'Lest the people change their minds when they see war and return to Egypt.' But God led the people round by the way of the wilderness towards the Red Sea.

God orchestrated this march based on His own perfect design for His people, teaching them to depend on Him to keep them on track, pilgrims on His way, learning to trust Him to meet their needs. The pilgrim life of God's people is not easy, then and now: but the difficulties we face are not evidence that He has abandoned us. Quite the opposite, in fact. We can't get to Sinai any other way![6]

Why is Sinai so important as the first destination for God's people? Two theological principles emerge through the story, principles at the heart of the covenant which God confirms with the people when they arrive at the mountain.

---

1. Exod. 14.
2. Exod. 15:22.
3. Exod. 16:1-3.
4. Exod. 17:1.
5. Exod. 17:8.
6. See Heb. 12:18-24: God's people are still journeying towards a mountain.

1. The place of law in the life of God's people. The sequence of events is absolutely vital for our understanding: first comes God's covenant commitment to His people, then the redemption from slavery, and then the law. In the Old Testament, therefore, the law is not a ladder whereby the unredeemed seek to climb into God's presence—to win His favour by pleasing Him. Rather, the law is a divinely-given pattern of life for those who have been redeemed because of *His prior* favour towards them. Remember how 'grace found Noah'? Here we have people who have rested underneath the sheltering blood of the Passover lamb, who are consequently bound to God as covenant pilgrims with Him, and who now arrive at the immediate objective of their pilgrimage—the place where they will hear God speak His word of law and commandment for them.

The law is thus the pattern of life which God sets before, and upon, His redeemed people. This is true throughout the Old Testament, and indeed in the New also. First grace, then law. One tiny New Testament example will illustrate the same pattern: Paul tells the Ephesians that they must:

> be imitators of God as beloved children. And walk in love, as Christ loved us and gave himself up for us, a fragrant offering and sacrifice to God. (Eph. 5:1-2)

You see the pattern? The Ephesians are already 'beloved children.' And as such they must imitate the God who has loved them, and specifically 'walk' (that pilgrim word again) in the love which Christ showed for them on the cross. As Christians we must increasingly ignore that blank page in our Bibles between Malachi and Matthew—the Bible speaks with one voice!

In both Testaments it is *God's own character*, revealed in the act of redemption, which forms the basis of the instruction then given. Here in Exodus, the law is first and foremost a revelation of God Himself, which then forms a pattern of life for the redeemed. God's own *character* is the basis of His *law*. To illustrate this, let's jump across for a moment from Exodus to Leviticus 19—a chapter which gathers together many diverse aspects of life and law: family life, the conduct of worship, farming practices, social relations including finance, how law courts should operate, sexual practices and attitudes to foreigners, etc. etc.! It is the chapter which includes the famous 'you shall love your neighbour as yourself' which Jesus quotes as one of the two greatest commandments on which 'depend all the Law and the Prophets.'[7] Note how this chapter starts:

> You shall be holy, for I the LORD your God am holy. (Lev. 19:2)

The purpose of God's law was to make His people holy like God Himself. Now notice the echo of this opening principle that rings through the chapter: 'I am the LORD' or 'I am the LORD your God' occurs no fewer than fifteen times attached to particular commandments, for instance:

> You shall not strip your vineyard bare, neither shall you gather the fallen grapes of your vineyard. You shall leave them for the poor and for the sojourner: I am the LORD your God. (Lev. 19:10)

> You shall not curse the deaf or put a stumbling block before the blind, but you shall fear your God: I am the LORD. (Lev. 19:14)

And finally, at the end of the chapter:

7. Lev. 19:18; Mark 12:31; Matt. 22:40.

> You shall observe all my statutes and all my rules, and do them: I am the LORD. (Lev. 19:37)

God reminds His people over and over again that these commandments are not arbitrary. They could no more be otherwise than God Himself could be otherwise—they translate His own character into practical behavioural form, reflecting the divine nature and designed to shape His people in His image. It's worth reflecting that, biblically, there are two images of God on earth: His image in humankind,[8] and His image in His law. This is true for 'the law' in both Testaments—both for the Mosaic law here in Exodus, and for what Paul calls 'the obedience of faith'.[9] In both cases, God's people are called to a lifestyle which will shape them into the 'likeness' of their God. God calls us New Testament believers to be 'conformed to the image of his Son' (Rom. 8:29)—to 'walk' in the love of the One who loved us on the cross. And this is, of course, how Paul can say that God's purpose was:

> that the righteous requirement of the law *[that is, the law of Moses]* might be fulfilled in us, who walk not according to the flesh but according to the Spirit. (Rom. 8:4)

The Holy Spirit within us, who is 'the Spirit of Christ' (Rom. 8:9), transforms us so that we take on the likeness of God's Son, and thus 'the law' is fulfilled in us too—because both the Lord Jesus, and the law of Moses, shine with God's image on earth, and by the Spirit we begin to shine too.[10] The same principle unites both

---

8. Gen. 1:26-27—a human image of course supremely manifested in the Lord Jesus, who is 'the image of the invisible God' (Col. 1:15).

9. Rom. 1:5, 16:26.

10. See also 2 Cor. 3:14-18. Of course there are some complications here, because we are not now required to obey all the details of the Mosaic law (see e.g. Mark 7:19). But the basic principle is clear!

Testaments: the law is what it is, because God is who He is, so that in turn we may become what God is. This is why Mount Sinai has such a central place in the covenant and in the total covenant document which is the Holy Scriptures.

Are you still with me? Hold this thought as we now look at the second vital theological principle which emerges in the Exodus Sinai story.

2. Approaching the unapproachable God through the blood of the covenant.

As we saw above, the Sinai narrative begins with God's summary of the story so far:

> You yourselves have seen what I did to the Egyptians, and how I bore you on eagles' wings and brought you to myself. (Exod. 19:4)

But how does this 'bringing to myself' actually work out? In the event, although the Israelites have arrived at Mount Sinai, they are kept back from coming face to face with God Himself. When God 'comes down' onto the mountain, the people are told to:

> Take care not to go up into the mountain or touch the edge of it. Whoever touches the mountain shall be put to death. (Exod. 19:12)

And when Moses climbs the mountain to meet God, God sends him back down immediately—

> Go down and warn the people, lest they break through to the LORD to look and many of them perish … do not let the priests and the people break through to come up to the LORD, lest he break out against them. (Exod. 19:21, 24)

How horrifying! And how strange. The people are brought near, but kept distant. Mount Sinai speaks with both a 'Yes' and a 'No' to God's people. We have met this before, in the Exodus story. Remember Moses' encounter with the burning bush?

> Moses said, 'I will turn aside to see this great sight, why the bush is not burned.' When the LORD saw that he turned aside to see, God called to him out of the bush, 'Moses, Moses!' And he said, 'Here am I.' Then he said, 'Do not come near.' (Exod. 3:3-5)

Moses comes close, but is kept back. Now Israel meets the burning bush on a grand scale—

> Now Mount Sinai was wrapped in smoke because the LORD had descended on it in fire. The smoke of it went up like the smoke of a kiln, and the whole mountain trembled greatly. (Exod. 19:18)

There is a wonderful continuity of biblical symbolism here! First Abraham saw it in a tiny form—the 'smoking firepot' that passed through the sacrifice.[11] Then Moses had a private preview when he saw the bush burning with the Lord's holy presence. Israel saw it enlarged into the pillar of fire that led the way for them every night, the Lord's visible presence with them, out in front.[12] Now they meet the full, awesome reality, with the whole mountain flaming, smoking and shaking. And in each case the humans involved come close—but not too close. God is with hHis people, revealing Himself, bringing them into relationship with Himself, but at the same time fencing them off.

So Sinai speaks with a double voice: 'Come and meet God! But … you can't actually meet Him.' Does this mean that, finally, the covenant relationship is impossible? All puff and no reality? This strange 'Yes, come to me; No,

11. Gen. 15:17.

12. Exod. 13:21 etc.

don't come to me' hangs over the narrative until we get to the covenant ratification ceremony that follows the giving of the law, in Exodus 24:

> And Moses wrote down all the words of the LORD. He rose early in the morning and built an altar at the foot of the mountain, and twelve pillars, according to the twelve tribes of Israel. And he sent young men of the people of Israel, who offered burnt offerings and sacrificed peace offerings of oxen to the LORD. And Moses took half of the blood and put it in basins, and half of the blood he threw against the altar. Then he took the Book of the Covenant and read it in the hearing of the people. And they said, 'All that the LORD has spoken we will do, and we will be obedient.' And Moses took the blood and threw it on the people and said, 'Behold the blood of the covenant which the LORD has made with you in accordance with all these words.' (Exod. 24:4-8)

Sacrifice makes the difference! We must look very carefully at what happens here. The altar with twelve pillars is a clear symbol: God, represented by the altar, is truly united with His people, represented by the twelve pillars. He has brought them to Himself, and they are gathered around Him. What enables this union is the blood of the sacrifice splashed against the altar. As we saw with the Passover, sacrificial blood exercises its influence chiefly towards God. His wrath is propitiated, and the holy God can be at peace with His people sheltering under the blood.

This is perhaps why the 'young men' offer just burnt offerings and peace offerings here. These are two of the three great offerings in the Levitical system—missing is the third, the sin offering, the offering which above all others made peace between sinners and a holy God. Effectively this peace was made for Israel at the

Passover: then sinners were saved into relationship with the Lord, and went walking with Him. Now that saving process is brought to completion with burnt offerings and peace offerings, together called 'the blood of the covenant'. The relationship is sealed!

But relationships have two sides. And biblical sacrifices work both towards God and towards us human beings. The other half of the sacrificial blood is thrown over the people as they commit themselves to follow and to obey:

> Then [Moses] took the Book of the Covenant and read it in the hearing of the people. And they said, 'All that the LORD has spoken we will do, and we will be obedient.' And Moses took the blood and threw it on the people and said, 'Behold the blood of the covenant which the LORD has made with you in accordance with all these words.' (Exod. 24:7-8)

We need to take careful note here of two things. Let's notice first *who* was splashed with the blood, and then secondly *when* the splashing took place:

- The *who*—God's covenant people, already on pilgrimage with Him, gathered at the foot of the mountain to which He has brought them.
- The *when*—at the moment of commitment, when they promise to be obedient to all they have heard.

Notice that the blood *follows* the commitment. They express their determination to obey the law they have just heard, and in response Moses throws the covenant blood over them. What does this mean? In a nutshell, it means that grace not only precedes law, it follows it as well. Both God and Moses know that the people are making a commitment way beyond their capacity. Looking back on this commitment years later, Moses says:

> And the LORD heard your words, when you spoke to me. And the LORD said to me, 'I have heard the words of this people, which they have spoken to you. Oh that they had such a mind as this always, to fear me and to keep all my commandments, that it might go well with them and with their descendants for ever!' (Deut. 5:28-29)

—but of course Israel does *not* have such a mind. Very soon, in the Exodus story—indeed, within days, while Moses is back up the mountain receiving further instructions—they will make a golden calf and start worshipping it.[13] Their commitment is only skin deep. As Hosea complains later, their 'love is like a morning cloud, like the dew that goes early away.'[14] Israel doesn't have the strength to keep this commitment. But grace *follows* law, so that when they fall into sin, the covenant blood will be there for them. The blood that *made* peace with God will also *keep* peace with God, when they stumble.

In our next chapter we will ask, 'How does the blood actually work?' But before we do that, here are two thoughts to round up this chapter:

(1) The shape of Old Testament religion. This pattern, grace–law–grace, is written deep into the way in which the Old Testament presents our relationship with God. We have seen this so clearly in the Exodus story—haven't we? We have seen the *grace* that brought Israel out of Egypt, the *law* that was then spoken to them because they were redeemed people, and the *grace* that

13. Exod. 32. 'They have turned aside quickly out of the way that I commanded them' (Exod. 32:8).

14. Hosea 6:4.

was immediately signalled to them as they committed themselves to a life of obedience.

It used to be fashionable for Old Testament specialists to say that there was a battle in ancient Israel between the priests and the prophets—between those who emphasised the sacrificial cult as the heart of religion (the priests), and those who emphasised the need for ethical obedience (the prophets). They could even point to places where the prophets seem to attack the cult as though it wasn't actually important or required.[15] But what the prophets hated was the *misuse* of the cult—in particular, when people just went through the motions of offering sacrifice, without true repentance of heart. The whole point of the sacrificial cult was to bring cleansing from sin, so that the cult tied together the blood of the sacrifice with commitment to obedience and ethical holiness. The prior call was to holiness, and then along came the sacrifices, to make provision for people's lapses. Grace–law–grace. There was no argument between the priests and the prophets!

(2) The unity of Old and New Testaments. We find exactly the same pattern of religion in the New Testament. We too, new covenant believers in Jesus, are called to holiness of life in commitment to Him—but He likewise makes 'grace' provision for us, if we lapse. For instance:

> My little children, I am writing these things to you so that you may not sin. But if anyone does sin, we have an advocate with the Father, Jesus Christ the righteous. He is the propitiation for our sins ... (1 John 2:1-2)

15. See e.g. Amos 5:21-24; Isa. 1:10-14; Jer. 6:20; Micah 6:6-8; Ps. 40:6-8.

Similarly, turning to Paul, it is instructive and encouraging to compare the first verse of Galatians 5 with the first verse of Galatians 6:

> For freedom Christ has set us free; stand firm therefore, and do not submit again to a yoke of slavery. (Gal. 5:1)

> Brothers, if anyone is caught in any transgression, you who are spiritual should restore him in a spirit of gentleness ... Bear one another's burdens, and so fulfil the law of Christ. (Gal 6:1-2)

As in Exodus, the 'law' of Christ is (a) to live in the freedom that He gives us, and (b) to encourage and restore one another, if we mess up. The law is not a ladder set before unbelievers, inviting them to struggle and strive up it towards heaven. The law is the pattern of life given to those who have been 'redeemed by the blood of the Lamb,'[16] so that they may be like their God. Notice the 'freedom' emphasis in Exodus, also: the law begins with God's declaration, 'I am the LORD your God, who brought you out of the land of Egypt, out of the house of slavery'[17]—or 'the house of bondage' as the older translations have it. The law that God gives is not a bondage, but a life for free people, designed to preserve them in that freedom.

At the heart of that freedom is the covenant relationship: God brings His people into committed relationship with Himself, He committed to them, they committed to Him. But we've already noticed the great tension at the heart of that relationship: He welcomes them to Himself, but they can't come into His holy presence. We noticed too that it is the *blood*—the 'blood of the covenant'—that makes the difference: focusing on

16. See Rev. 5:9.

17. Exod. 20:2.

God in propitiation, and on the people in preservation, maintaining them in fellowship with God. So let's now look more closely at the blood and ask, How does it work?

4

Covenant and Sacrifice —onward from Sinai

Again, let's do an action replay of the story so far.

- God's covenant commitment to rescue the world from sin, death and confusion, betokened in the story of Noah, is focused onto
- His promise to Abraham to be in permanent covenant relationship with his family, which in turn leads to
- His rescue of Israel from slavery in Egypt, which more importantly turns out to be His rescue from the death which is the consequence of His own wrath against sin and disobedience.
- That first Passover launches God's people into pilgrimage with Him. The journey is both *with* and *to* the Lord—He leads and accompanies them on their way, and brings them *to Himself* at Mount Sinai.
- At Sinai the people draw close to God but are also kept away from Him—any closer, and they would be destroyed.

- The law is given to guide and shape their life reflecting God's own character, and they commit themselves to their side of the covenant—but we know that their commitment is only skin deep.
- What ensures their on-going safety in this perilous relationship with their covenant God is 'the blood of the covenant' which Moses throws over them as they commit themselves to obedience—but how does this blood actually work?

That's the question we are left with, in Exodus 24. Immediately after the covenant ratification ceremony in 24:3-8, we are given a wonderful token of the *effectiveness* of the blood:

> Then Moses and Aaron, Nadab, and Abihu, and seventy of the elders of Israel went up, and they saw the God of Israel. There was under his feet as it were a pavement of sapphire stone, like the very heaven for clearness. And he did not lay his hand on the chief men of the people of Israel; they beheld God, and ate and drank. (Exod. 24:9-11)

Can you sense how amazing this is? Represented by their elders, Israel is now invited into the very presence of God, who does not 'break out against them' as they were warned earlier.[1] There is mutual seeing, and table fellowship together. That 'throwing' of the blood, first onto the altar and then onto the people, has clearly worked wonders. Is this how it is going to be, from now on? Sadly, no. But this story *betokens* what life is like, when God's wrath is propitiated and God's people are protected by the blood of the covenant. And it points forward to the outcome of the 'new covenant', energised by the life-giving Spirit in Christ, whereby:

---

1. Exod. 19:24.

> we all, with unveiled face, beholding the glory of the Lord, are being transformed into the same image ... For God ... has shone in our hearts to give the light of the knowledge of the glory of God in the face of Jesus Christ.[2]

In our next chapter we will look forward to the new covenant, in both Old and New Testaments. Here we focus on the question: how does *the blood* achieve that intimate fellowship between God and human beings pictured in Exodus 24? This is a vital question, which will help us in due course to understand the cross of Christ. To dig deeper into it, we must look at where the book of Exodus goes next, after Sinai, and how it leads into Leviticus.

The second half of Exodus is taken up with the tabernacle and its arrangements—its design, construction, ministry and consecration.[3] Why this focus? Exodus 29:44-46 gives us the underlying theology:

> *[The LORD said to Moses]* 'I will consecrate the tent of meeting and the altar. Aaron also and his sons I will consecrate to serve me as priests. I will dwell among the people of Israel and I will be their God. And they shall know that I am the LORD their God, who brought them out of the land of Egypt that I might dwell among them. I am the LORD their God.'

Notice carefully here (a) the *basic covenant commitment* ('I will be their God'), (b) the *expression* of this commitment in God's plan to 'dwell among' His people—the whole purpose of the exodus from Egypt—and (c) the *focus* of this 'dwelling' in the tabernacle, called

2. 2 Cor. 3:18, 4:6; cf. 3:6.

3. With an interlude in chapters 32–34 for the golden calf episode, which reminds us how much the people needed God's unfailing commitment to the covenant, represented by the provision of the tabernacle and the sacrifices in it.

'the tent of meeting'. The tabernacle is the climax of the redemption story so far, because it is the visible expression of the covenant: God is moving into the street, pitching His tent among all the other tents, getting an address just down the road from everyone else in the camp of Israel.

How much people must have looked forward to God's moving-in day! But when it comes, glorious though it is, we crash into the same disappointment as earlier:

> Then the cloud covered the tent of meeting, and the glory of the LORD filled the tabernacle. And Moses was not able to enter the tent of meeting because the cloud settled on it, and the glory of the LORD filled the tabernacle. (Exod. 40:34-35)

How tragic, and how ironic! The tabernacle is called 'the tent of meeting', but even Moses can't meet Him. The cloud of God's presence is now in the midst of the people, but the cloud keeps people out. God has moved in next door, but He's not a neighbour.

How can this terrible irony be resolved? Finally it won't be sorted out until, through the cross, 'a new and living way' is opened up for us so that 'we have confidence to enter the holy places by the blood of Jesus'.[4] Ultimately, within biblical theology, only the blood of Christ gives us unfenced access to the immediate presence of God. But this teasing question with which we are left, at the end of Exodus, is addressed straightaway by the laws about sacrifice in Leviticus. Notice how Leviticus begins:

> The LORD called Moses and spoke to him from the tent of meeting, saying 'Speak to the people of Israel and say to them, "When any one of you brings an offering to the LORD …"' (Lev. 1:1-2)

---

4. Heb. 10:19-20.

A literal translation here would be, 'When any one of you *brings near that which is brought near* ...' The sacrifices are about enabling the people to *come near,* even though they cannot enter. The sacrifices are designed to maintain God's redeemed people in fellowship with Him—living in the same street—even though they can't pile into His living room.

The first Passover in Egypt was the basic, unrepeatable covenant sacrifice that launched Israel into life on the road with their God. Thereafter, the sacrifices maintain the redeemed in fellowship with their God. So the Passover is the model of the 'one sacrifice for sins for ever,' as Hebrews describes the cross.[5] The Passover could only be sacrificed in Egypt, because it was designed to get the people out of there. Thereafter, the Levitical sacrifices maintained them in their new pilgrimage with their God. Similarly the cross is the single unrepeatable sacrifice which brings us into God's presence, but at the same time 'the blood of Jesus His Son keeps on cleansing us from all sin' when we need it.[6]

The sacrifices could not be offered by non-Israelites. They could only be offered by people who stood under that initial, redeeming sacrifice. If someone wanted to join Israel, there were two requirements: circumcision, and participation in the Passover. The annual repetition of the Passover was meant to re-appropriate and reaffirm the people's participation in that initial redemption—and a Gentile could join at that point. Thereafter, once brought into the redeemed people, Gentiles could offer sacrifices and thus be maintained in God's fellowship, 'bringing near that which is brought near'. All the

5. Heb. 10:12, the older translations. ESV has 'for all time a single sacrifice for sins'.

6. 1 John 1:7, literal translation.

sacrifices in Leviticus—burnt offerings, peace offerings and sin offerings—are summarised under this initial description: they are about 'bringing near that which is brought near'.

The sacrificial system was complex, and we don't need to harness all the details in our exploration of their underlying covenant theology. For our purposes there were two features of all the sacrifices, of whatever type, which help us to pull out their meaning: (a) the offerers had to lay their hands on the head of the offering, and (b) there was always a ceremonial action to deal with the blood shed when the sacrificial animal was killed. If we look at each of these, we will begin to get a sense of the meaning of the sacrifices, and in particular begin to understand why the *blood* is so important, and how it works. We are on a glorious biblical quest.

1. The laying-on of hands.

This is required for all three types of offering in Leviticus. We first meet it in the burnt offering regulations:

> He shall lay his hand on the head of the burnt offering, and it shall be accepted for him to make atonement for him. (Lev. 1:4)

The same applies to the peace offering[7] and the sin offering.[8] The laying-on of hands is a symbol with a meaning, and to discover its meaning we can helpfully glance across to Numbers, to the regulations surrounding the consecration of the Levites to serve in the tabernacle. We read that

> When you bring the Levites before the LORD, the people of Israel shall lay their hands on the Levites.[9]

7. Lev. 3:2.
8. Lev. 4:4.
9. Num. 8:10.

—and the meaning of this action then emerges in the verses that follow:

> Aaron shall offer the Levites before the LORD as a wave offering from the people of Israel, that they may do the service of the LORD ... Thus you shall separate the Levites from among the people of Israel, and the Levites shall be mine ... For they are wholly given to me from among the people of Israel. Instead of all who open the womb, the firstborn of all the people of Israel, I have taken them for myself. For all the firstborn among the people of Israel are mine, both of man and of beast. On the day that I struck down all the firstborn in the land of Egypt I consecrated them for myself, and I have taken the Levites instead of all the firstborn among the people of Israel.[10]

Notice the repeated phrase 'instead of'. God consecrates the Levites to His service instead of taking all the first-born, and it is this 'instead of' relationship which is expressed when 'the people of Israel' are involved in the consecration ceremony. The laying-on of hands thus appointed the Levites to stand in a certain relationship to the people who performed it—they were set apart to act in their place, to fulfil service on their behalf.

Returning to Leviticus, let's bring into the picture the ceremony of the Day of Atonement, where we read that

> Aaron shall lay both his hands on the head of the live goat, and confess over it all the iniquities of the people of Israel, and all their transgressions, all their sins ... The goat shall bear all their iniquities on itself ...[11]

Here the laying-on of hands signifies the transference of sin and guilt. So when worshippers made offerings and laid their hands on the head of the sacrificial

10. Num. 8:11, 14, 16-18.

11. Lev. 16:21-22.

animal, what did the action mean? The animal was being appointed to stand in their place, and (especially in the case of the sin offering) to bear their sins and transgressions instead of them. The laying-on of hands symbolises the appointment of a substitute, who then goes to death *instead of* the worshipper.

This is a vital principle in biblical theology: the principle of *sacrificial substitution*. It underlies the New Testament presentation of the cross. For instance, the little expression 'on behalf of' is used in the New Testament no fewer than thirty-six times with reference to the death of the Lord Jesus 'for' us.[12] Jesus stands in for us, dying on our behalf as our substitute under God's wrath, bearing the penalty of our sin.

So, following on from this, what can we say about the significance of the sacrificial blood?

2. The meaning of the blood.

There is a vital passage later in Leviticus which unpacks this for us—one of only a few in the Old Testament which explain how the sacrifices work. There was a strong prohibition against eating blood as a food,[13] and Leviticus 17:11 gives the reason for this:

> For the life of the flesh is in the blood, and I have given it for you on the altar to make atonement for your souls, for it is the blood that makes atonement by the life.

---

12. See for instance Mark 14:24, John 10:15, Rom. 5:6, Gal. 2:20, Heb. 2:9—etc. For the technically minded, this is the Greek preposition *huper*: see the very useful little discussion by Dr Leon Morris in *The Apostolic Preaching of the Cross* (London: Tyndale Press, 1955), pp. 62-64.

13. 'If any one of the house of Israel or of the strangers who sojourn among them eats any blood, I will set my face against that person ... and will cut him off from among his people' (Lev. 17:10).

This is quite a condensed explanation of the 'working' of the blood. Let's focus on four aspects of this important statement.

(1) 'The life of the flesh is in the blood.' It's not obvious in the English translations, but the Hebrew word for 'life'—the great word *nephesh*—actually occurs three times here: translated twice as 'life', and once as 'souls'. *Nephesh* means 'soul, living being, life, self, person, desire, appetite, emotion, and passion'.[14] As you can see, it has a wide range of meaning, summarising the *aliveness* of living beings, all that distinguishes us as *alive* from bodies from which life has departed. When God breathed 'the breath of life' into him, Adam became a 'living *nephesh*' (Gen. 2:7), and the same phrase ('living *nephesh*') is used of all *animal* life in Genesis 1:30.[15]

Leviticus 17:11 now tells us that it is not just *breath* which distinguishes all animate life, and marks us as 'living' no, it is *blood*. The flesh-life of all of us, humans and animals alike, is carried and symbolised by our blood, which contains and energises the livingness of our bodies. So when blood is shed, life ends, unless radical action is taken to stem the flow. But in the case of the animal sacrifices—and in the case of Jesus' sacrificial death on the cross—this is deliberate shedding of blood, aimed at killing. The blood flows, and life ends, as a payment for the sins of others. The 'life' of the sacrifice is laid down, to make atonement for the 'lives' of others: one *nephesh* in substitution for others.

---

14. This is the summary of the range of meaning of *nephesh*, given by Brown, Driver and Briggs in their famous Hebrew dictionary (Brown, Driver and Briggs, *Hebrew and English Lexicon of the Old Testament* (Oxford: Clarendon Press, 1972), p. 659).

15. ESV translates the phrase 'every living *nephesh*' as 'everything that has the breath of life', cf. Gen. 2:19, where 'every living creature' is the same phrase in the Hebrew.

(2) 'I have given it for you on the altar.' This is a most important feature which distinguishes the biblical sacrifices from all others. In all other religions where they occur, animal sacrifices (and indeed all kinds of sacrifice) are a human expedient, designed to placate an angry deity, influence the course of events, achieve a desired goal, or avert a disaster. But the biblical sacrifices are not a human expedient; they are a divine provision—'I have given it for you.' God Himself has decided that sacrificial blood, representing a *nephesh* laid down in death, can be substituted for our *nephesh,* so that we can live and not die. This gives biblical sacrifices both a unique *origin* (God's will and decision[16]) and a unique *purpose* (one life is laid down for another).

(3) 'To make atonement for your souls.' The word translated 'make atonement' has the consistent meaning 'to pay a ransom price', 'to make a payment designed to discharge an indebtedness'. The blood achieves its substitutionary effect by making a payment to discharge a debt. Actually the basic meaning of the verb is 'to cover'. To understand this biblically we might think of the Israelites 'covered' by the blood of the Passover, sheltering behind their doors smeared with blood. Or imagine you come to pay the bill at the end of your meal, and the waiter says, 'Don't worry—the bill's been covered by that gentleman over there,' and you look round to see an old friend smiling at you. A payment has been made to cover your indebtedness.

The Passover is the true biblical illustration. On Passover night the penalty of sin was death, and the payment which discharged that indebtedness was the life of the lamb laid down in death. The efficacy of

---

16. cf. John 6:50-51; Acts 2:23; Rom. 8:3-4; Gal. 4:4; 2 Cor. 5:21—verses all underlining the origin of the cross in the will of God.

that death—through which Israel was launched into pilgrimage with her covenant God—is *prolonged* into the three-fold system of sacrifices in Leviticus, which likewise make atonement by 'covering' the debt owed by the worshippers, whether it's the debt arising from their sinful disobedience (the sin offerings), or from their total indebtedness to the Lord their Creator God (the burnt offerings), or from their need to live in closer relationship with God and each other (the peace offerings). The blood thus signifies a life laid down *instead of* the life of the one who brings the offering, to discharge the debt arising from our constant falling short in all these areas.

(4) 'For it is the blood that makes atonement by the life.' Here the last phrase ('by the life') is really important. Some Old Testament theologians used to argue that the point of the shedding of blood was not to effect a death, but to release a life: the idea was, they said, that the life released from the victim could then be transferred to, or absorbed by, the offerer. Death meant the liberation of a life to be shared with others. Does this make sense? These last words in Leviticus 17:11 might seem to support this understanding of sacrifice.[17] But as we have seen, behind these words lies a long story which starts with the Passover, and there the death of the lamb did not mean the release of a life—no more than did the death of all the first-born in Egypt. Death was then, and still is, what Paul calls 'the wages of sin'[18]—the consequence, under God's judgment, of disobedience to His word and law. The payment that discharges our indebtedness is the payment of a life laid

17. This is all brilliantly set out and discussed by Leon Morris in the book referred to above, *The Apostolic Preaching of the Cross*, pp. 112-128.

18. Rom. 6:23.

down in death, exactly as the Passover lamb was the dead one, in each Israelite household on Passover night.

Furthermore, the phrase 'by the life' has an important legal connection. We find this phrase also in Deuteronomy 19:21, where Moses announces a fundamental legal principle to be applied by judges when sentencing:

> Your eye shall not pity. It shall be life for life, eye for eye, tooth for tooth, hand for hand, foot for foot.

The Hebrew preposition 'for', used here, expresses exact equivalence, and is often used in commercial transactions as well as legal contexts: the money paid or goods exchanged have to be the exact equivalent 'for' the value or price of the items bought. Apply this thought to the use of the same preposition in Leviticus 19:11: it would fit if we translated this last clause 'for it is the blood that makes atonement *at the expense of* the life.' The life is laid down as the equivalent, in God's economy, of the life of the sinner who repents and brings the offering.

Let's draw the threads together. We conclude that the sacrifices were a divine provision to maintain God's redeemed people in fellowship with Him. They did this by prolonging the virtues and the meaning of the initial Passover sacrifice, where life went for life and, on the basis of substitution, God's wrath was propitiated and God's people were made secure. The blood symbolised life poured out into death, so that God's people might not die in their sins, but live in peace with their God and with each other.

Before we end this chapter, however, let's draw a line across to a famous New Testament passage that draws on Leviticus 17:10-11, and which helps us to apply all these thoughts to the death of our Lord Jesus. In John

6, at the end of His famous 'Bread of Life' sermon, Jesus shocks His hearers by apparently turning on its head the prohibition on eating blood, and applying it to Himself in a very personal way:

> Truly, truly, I say to you, unless you eat the flesh of the Son of Man and drink his blood, you have no life in you. Whoever feeds on my flesh and drinks my blood has eternal life, and I will raise him up on the last day. For my flesh is true food, and my blood is true drink. Whoever feeds on my flesh and drinks my blood abides in me, and I in him. As the living Father sent me, and I live because of the Father, so whoever feeds on me, he also will live because of me.[19]

We notice the same connection between 'blood' and 'life'—the Leviticus 17 principle. But at first sight, Jesus seems to be affirming the view of sacrifice which we rejected a moment ago, namely that sacrifice is about releasing a life which others can then share: because He has died, His life—which is the life of God His Father—can be 'in' us, if we 'feed on' Him. So feed on Him we must, if we are to have eternal life! Are we meeting a different view of sacrifice here? In response we must say No!—and make two comments:

(1) This picture of 'eating' the sacrifice reflects the experience of every Israelite family, who would normally feed together on the meat of their peace offerings, after it had been offered—reflecting, of course, the eating of the Passover lamb. They ate in gladness for the sacrifice, aware that the sacrificial animal had died so that they might live in fellowship with God and each other.[20] This is the base-line in John 6 also.

---

19. John 6:53-57.

20. See Lev. 7:15-18. The burnt offerings were wholly burnt—nothing was eaten (Lev. 1:9)—and the priests alone were allowed to eat parts of the sin offerings (Lev. 7:6).

But, (2) Jesus is adding an extra to this picture, because of the glorious truth that He, our Saviour, having shed His blood for us, rose from the dead and now comes to live within us by His Spirit. Our salvation rests not just on the effectiveness of His death for us, but on the reality of His resurrection for us, too. He performs both actions, both His death and His resurrection, on our behalf. As Paul says, 'he was delivered up for our trespasses and raised for our justification.'[21] In the Old Testament, sacrificial cult worshippers laid their hands on the animal to symbolise their identification with its death, as we saw. We are identified with the Lord Jesus even more intimately, because the Holy Spirit unites us with Him, so that a great exchange takes place: He takes our sin and death, and we receive His resurrected life. Paul loves to emphasise the truth that we both die and rise with the Lord Jesus.[22]

And that resurrection life is not just a matter of future hope. As we can see so vividly in John 6, Jesus' life in us is a matter of feeding on Him now, by faith, so that we ingest Him and digest Him and absorb Him into the very marrow of our being. We feed on His flesh and His blood in which is eternal life for us, both now and after death. This truth is so glorious and so new, going beyond the Old Testament theology of sacrifice, that only Jesus' shocking words about 'drinking blood' are sufficient to express it.

Will you take a moment now to reflect on these glorious truths for yourself? Viewed in this whole-Bible perspective, the covenant sacrifices take us to the heart of what it means to be God's people: flawed and frail, sinful and subject to death, we are rescued and raised

21. Rom. 4:25.

22. See e.g. Rom. 6:4-5; Col. 2:12-13.

by a God who *Himself* becomes the sacrifice for us, and calls us into intimate, daily communion with His Son our Saviour.

It is fitting that we have jumped over into the New Testament at the end of this chapter because now we need to turn to the ways in which the Old Testament looks ahead to a *new* covenant yet to be. That's where our journey takes us next.

5

The Covenant to Come –the need for something more

Thus far, we have been considering the covenant foundations laid through Abraham and Moses, which shaped the heart of Israel's relationship with God. But we have already noticed the weevil in the biscuit—Israel's capacity to rebel, even within days of their loud commitment to obedience at Sinai. What can be done about this? Where is this all heading? What more can, or must, be done in order to make the covenant work? Join me as we seek to discover the answers in our remaining chapters together.

We can summarise our destination under the heading 'the perfection yet to be'. The Old Testament envisages a coming perfection of the covenant. It was Jeremiah who first used the expression 'a new covenant' to express this,[1] but the idea is much more widespread than the expression. Moses first plants the idea, in what looks like very unpromising ground—as you will immediately gather from the first of our two main headings in this chapter.

1. Jer. 31:31.

1. The vengeance, or curse, of the covenant. Strangely (indeed, wonderfully) the envisaged coming perfection of the covenant is rooted in God's promise of vengeance upon those who break it. This appears in two main passages in the Pentateuch. We turn first to Leviticus 26, where the Lord first describes the blessings that will follow from obedience (vv. 3-13) climaxing with the fulfilment of the great covenant promise:

> And I will walk among you and will be your God, and you shall be my people. I am the LORD your God, who brought you out of the land of Egypt, that you should not be their slaves. And I have broken the bars of your yoke and made you walk erect. (Lev. 26:12-13)

But on the other hand, if they spurn His statutes, abhor His rules, fail to keep His commandments and 'break my covenant' (v. 15), then all sorts of curses will follow (vv. 16-39), which will include defeat by their enemies and the loss of the land the Lord is giving them. The nub of the curse is expressed in verse 25:

> And I will bring a sword upon you, that shall execute vengeance for the covenant.

The older Revised Version renders this more directly and truly:

> And I will bring a sword upon you, that shall execute the vengeance of the covenant.

In other words, God is not taking vengeance on behalf of a covenant which now lies in ruins. Rather, He is exacting vengeance *within* the covenant. In taking vengeance on His disobedient people, He is *keeping* His side of the covenant commitment. This is such an important point to grasp: on *God's* side, there is no repudiation of the covenant. The vengeance is not alien to the covenant, nor does it nullify it, but *belongs to* it.

Leviticus 26 goes on both to reveal the heart of the problem, and to show what further action God will take, to keep the covenant. After describing the terrible consequences of Israel's 'treachery that they committed against me … so that I walked contrary to them and brought them into the land of their enemies' (vv. 40-41), the LORD continues:

> if then their uncircumcised heart is humbled and they make amends for their iniquity, then I will remember my covenant with Jacob, and I will remember my covenant with Isaac and my covenant with Abraham, and I will remember the land … (Lev. 26:41-42)

Join me in noticing two things here:

- On the one hand, the root cause of the problem is Israel's 'uncircumcised heart'—somehow the covenant relationship, signalled by bodily circumcision, has not sunk deep into the place where it really matters;
- On the other hand, God's response is 'business as usual' in His commitment to the covenant—they may forget, but He will 'remember'.

He goes on:

> Yet for all that, when they are in the land of their enemies, I will not spurn them, neither will I abhor them so as to destroy them utterly and break my covenant with them, for I am the LORD their God. But I will for their sake remember the covenant with their forefathers, whom I brought out of the land of Egypt in the sight of the nations, that I might be their God: I am the LORD. (Lev. 26:44-45)

In the very situation where the vengeance of the covenant is in operation because of the uncircumcised heart, God has by no means abandoned His purposes or come to the end of His resources. His people may break the covenant, but He will not. 'Yahweh'—'the LORD'—is the name of the covenant God: His name does not change, and therefore the covenant is for ever secure at His end. The assured future for the covenant is built-in, even when God must talk of 'vengeance.'

Or indeed, of 'the curse'. Come with me now to Deuteronomy 29. Israel is in Moab, about to enter the promised land, and once again God marks the moment by renewing the covenant with His people. Moses tells them that they are standing before the LORD:

> so that you may enter into the sworn covenant of the LORD your God, which the LORD your God is making with you today. (Deut. 29:12)

Here we must engage in a little re-translation. The Hebrew literally says, 'so that you may enter into the covenant of the LORD your God and into his curse.' This is a very striking expression. The covenant is identified with 'a curse', because the human participants already know that, if they violate it, then the 'curses' will fall—the curses promised by the covenant itself. So we hear, just a few verses later, that if any one turns away from the LORD in their heart to serve other gods:

> the curses written in this book will settle upon [that person] ... and the LORD will single him out from all the tribes of Israel for calamity, in accordance with all the curses of the covenant written in this Book of the Law. (Deut. 29:20-21)

Notice that striking phrase, 'the curses of the covenant'. The covenant is not broken *by God* when Israel falls under the curses, which are laid out so vividly in Deuteronomy 28–29. Far from it. The curses come because God is *keeping* the covenant.

But is that the only envisaged future of the covenant? Certainly not. After the rain comes the sun:

> And when all these things come upon you, the blessing and the curse, which I have set before you, and you call them to mind among all the nations where the LORD your God has driven you, and return to the LORD your God, you and your children, and obey his voice in all that I command you this day, with all your heart and with all your soul, then the LORD your God will restore your fortunes ... (Deut. 30:1-3)

Specifically, He will gather the people from exile (v. 4), bring them back to the land they lost (v. 5a), make them prosperous again (v. 5b), and supremely:

> The LORD your God will circumcise your heart and the heart of your offspring, so that you will love the LORD your God with all your heart and with all your soul, that you may live. (Deut. 30:6)

The defect noticed in Leviticus (the uncircumcised heart) will be put right. The LORD envisages a covenant action reaching into the place unreached before, the rebellious heart, so that His people will be brought into new covenant blessing. This, as we'll see below in chapter 7, is the core of Jeremiah's 'new covenant' prophecy: and it's also the core of Paul's happy declaration that

> if you confess with your mouth that Jesus is Lord and believe in your heart that God raised him from the dead, you will be saved. For with the heart one believes and is justified, and with the mouth one confesses and is saved.[2]

Saving faith means a saved, believing heart! Israel's problem, as we saw, was that their dramatic confession of loyalty in Exodus 24 was not matched by an inner

2. Rom. 10:9-10.

reorientation around obedience and trust. In the Gospel, Paul is delighted to declare, that problem is solved.

But in the Old Testament, the curses of the covenant were built into the historical life of God's people. On entering the promised land, they were commanded to identify two mountains with, respectively, the blessings and the curses of the covenant. Two fixed, immovable features of the landscape were to remind them of the two ways the covenant could be expressed towards them: Mount Gerizim was identified with the blessings, and Mount Ebal with the curses.[3] Notice that these mountains do not represent obedience and disobedience, but the *results* of obedience or disobedience. They stand for the fixed, immovable covenant, which, without changing its nature, can bring either blessing or vengeance.

Notice with me a most beautiful touch in Deuteronomy 27 and Joshua 8, where the set-up of these two mountains is specified: Mount Ebal is identified with cursing, but it is on Mount Ebal that the altar is to be built.[4] The altar is not built in the place of blessing, but in the place representing God's curse. By setting it up in this way, God identifies Himself with the falling of His own curse—and this reaches right back to the institution of the covenant with Abraham, when it was God alone who marched between the severed carcasses and thereby took upon Himself the total obligation of the broken covenant. Right at the point of failure, Moses quietly hints at the coming perfection of the covenant, and thus points us forward to the supreme place where the covenant God will become a curse for His people—see Galatians 3:13.

---

3. See Deut. 11:26-30.

4. See Deut. 27:4-8; Josh. 8:30-32.

The covenant thus stands firm, even when—indeed, *especially* when—the curses fall on disobedience.

We need to add a footnote here concerning the prophet Amos. His were the first prophecies to be written down, and it used to be maintained that the reason for this was that Amos dared to predict the *termination* of the covenant relationship. Old Testament scholars argued that the 'hopeful' passage with which Amos ends (Amos 9:11-15) was added by a later scribe, who could not bear the horror of Amos' stark and hopeless message. Amos taught (so they said) that Israel's sin was so great that the covenant was irrevocably broken, and a final, irreversible judgment was on its way. For instance, Amos 9:1-10 is headed 'The destruction of Israel' in ESV, and it certainly looks final:

> Strike the capitals until the thresholds shake, and shatter them on the heads of all the people; and those who are left of them I will kill with the sword; not one of them shall flee away; not one of them shall escape ... And if they go into captivity before their enemies, there I will command the sword, and it shall kill them; and I will fix my eyes upon them for evil and not for good. (Amos 9:1, 4)

Amos apparently envisages not restoration for the people in exile, but termination: an awful end at the hands of a God who intends evil towards them rather than good. Is this really the end of the covenant? We need to read Amos very carefully: in fact (as in Deuteronomy) he binds the hope of restoration tightly within this terrible expectation of judgment. For instance:

> Behold, the eyes of the Lord GOD are upon the sinful kingdom, and I will destroy it from the surface of the ground, except that I will not utterly destroy the house of Jacob, declares the LORD. (Amos 9:8)

There is clearly a difference between 'destroy' and 'utterly destroy'! Following 'destruction' there will be restoration—

> In that day I will raise up the booth of David that is fallen and repair its breaches, and raise up its ruins and rebuild it as in the days of old ... (Amos 9:11)[5]

In fact we meet in Amos exactly what we have found in Leviticus and Deuteronomy: the future of the covenant contains both cursing and blessing. Without changing its nature, the covenant can bring either blessing or vengeance to God's people: and, say both Moses and Amos, it *will* bring both.

Where does this leave us, as New Covenant believers? Can we too fall under cursing as well as blessing? We will turn to this most important question later—store it up for now. In the meantime we will continue to trace the story of the covenant in the Old Testament as we notice:

2. The failure of the covenant institutions.

Throughout the story of the covenant, it was at the point of failure that hope was prompted. And this is true also as we look at the great institutions that were meant to secure the covenant relationship, and keep Israel safe. I'm going to look at two of these more briefly, and then dwell in much greater detail on a third. In fact, the third will take us forward into the next chapter.

(1) The covenant priesthood.

Within the main covenant with Israel, there was a particular covenant which God made with the priesthood. The priests, above all, were meant to act to preserve

---

5. See Acts 15:15-17, where James quotes this passage from Amos, declaring that it has been fulfilled through Jesus and through the preaching of the Gospel.

Israel from sin, by both preventative and restorative means: by acting to steer them away from sin, and by administering the sacrifices if they failed. We see this illustrated vividly in Numbers 25, where Phineas the priest was 'jealous with my jealousy'[6] and took dramatic action to stop the Israelites from intermarrying with the local Moabite population. As a result, Phineas was given a special covenant of his own:

> Behold, I give to him my covenant of peace, and it shall be to him and to his descendants after him the covenant of a perpetual priesthood, because he was jealous for his God and made atonement for the people of Israel. (Num. 25:12-13)

However—tracing the story through the Old Testament—the priests allowed their special covenant and privilege to be corrupted into a superstitious ritualism, and as a result came under sharp criticism from the prophets. We noticed some of these passages earlier.[7] The prophets often criticised the priests for losing the heart of their ministry, just as they also inveighed against false prophets for leading the people astray.[8]

At the very end of the prophetic movement Malachi looks at the priesthood in his day, and finds them very far from the priesthood that God intended. He mourns over the situation. He celebrates what once was, and should still be:

> My covenant with [Levi] was one of life and peace ... it was a covenant of fear, and he feared me. He stood in awe of my name. True instruction was in his mouth, and no wrong was found on his lips. He walked with

6. Num. 25:11.

7. See above, pp [50, 51] and chapter 3, footnote [15].

8. See e.g. Jer. 2:8, 23:11; Lam. 4:13; Ezek. 22:26; Hosea 4:4-6, 6:9; Micah. 3:11-12.

> me in peace and uprightness, and he turned many from iniquity. For the lips of a priest should guard knowledge, and people should seek instruction from his mouth, for he is the messenger of the LORD of hosts. (Mal. 2:5-7)

But things are sadly different from this ideal:

> But you have turned aside from the way. You have caused many to stumble by your instruction. You have corrupted the covenant of Levi, says the LORD of hosts. (Mal. 2:8)

The priests had not only corrupted their God-given rituals into superstition, but they had abandoned and corrupted their task of teaching the people. The covenant institution of the priesthood was a failure.

(2) The covenant institution of the tabernacle (and of the temple, as it later became).

Tabernacle and temple were—as we've seen—the symbolic focus of the achievement of the covenant goal, the indwelling of God among His people guaranteeing their security. But we've also seen the tension at the heart of this achievement: God is present, but also unapproachably separate. Can tabernacle and temple really—ever—solve this dilemma?

Let's turn to Zechariah for a perspective on this. Israel has returned from exile to a ruined Jerusalem and temple, and after a stuttering start Zechariah and Haggai were instrumental in gingering a rebuilding campaign off the ground. In chapter 2, Zechariah sees an enthusiastic young man rushing out with measuring line, 'to measure Jerusalem, to see what is its width and what is its length' (v. 2). He is measuring Jerusalem for a new suit—a new wall—perfectly matching the dimensions of the old city. He wants to determine the future by the measurements of the past, recreating the glory of David and Solomon, and enclosing God's people within the security of a rebuilt wall, alongside a rebuilt temple.

To this Zechariah responds with a resounding 'No!'—because, he says, there is a coming glory which will outshine and outmeasure anything that has gone before. Jerusalem does not need a wall, because:

> I will be to her a wall of fire all around, declares the LORD, and I will be the glory in her midst ... Sing and rejoice, O daughter of Zion, for behold I come and I will dwell in your midst, declares the LORD. And many nations shall join themselves to the LORD in that day, and shall be my people. And I will dwell in your midst ... (Zech. 2:5, 10-11)

Notice the triple 'in her/your midst'! The very failure, the destruction, of the tabernacle and temple says that something more is needed. There is a covenant perfection yet to be, which was not realised in the old institutions, or they would not have fallen. We are touching into a great mystery at the heart of biblical theology here. Of course part of the reason for their fall was that the people had corrupted them—remember Jeremiah's powerful accusation, later quoted by Jesus, that they had made the house of God into 'a den of robbers'.[9] A den of robbers is a place into which an ungodly, immoral, dishonest person runs for safety, and from which he emerges utterly unchanged. The people fled into this port of reformation and came out unreformed, ready to carry on their godless ways—this was Jeremiah's charge. They thought that God's house could be used without reference to moral reformation.

9. Jer. 7:11; Mark 11:17.

So the failure of the covenant institution is bound up with the failure that arises from the corruption of the human heart. But we need more than just a transformed heart in God's people. There is also a need for a fuller, more complete and more operative indwelling of God, an indwelling which will truly display the holiness of the God 'in their midst', in a way not possible within the old physical institutions. Something new is coming, which the Old Testament does not specify in detail, even though the vision of the perfect temple shines out so clearly. For instance, in the teaching of Micah:

> Because of you Zion shall be ploughed as a field, Jerusalem shall become a heap of ruins, and the mountain of the house a wooded height. It shall come to pass in the latter days that the mountain of the house of the LORD shall be established as the highest of the mountains, and it shall be lifted up above the hills; and peoples shall flow to it, and many nations shall come, and say: 'Come, let us go up to the mountain of the LORD, to the house of the God of Jacob, that he may teach us his ways, and that we may walk in his paths.' For out of Zion shall go forth the law, and the word of the LORD from Jerusalem. (Micah 3:12–4:2)

Notice how, for both Micah and Zechariah, this new temple will be for all the nations, and not just for Israel. Far from shrinking, the vision *grew* in response to the loss of the temple in Jerusalem, even though the glory had never been fully and properly realised there. To discover exactly what this glorious new temple-for-all-the-world will look like, we have to wait for the New Testament vision of the church as God's temple, indwelt by the Holy Spirit, its doors flung open to all comers, the home of the Good News and the place where never-ending worship rises to His glory.[10]

(3) The covenant institution of monarchy.

Old Testament kingship is another institution, and theme, which is vital within Old Testament Covenant Theology and which feeds through into the New Testament vision of the Lord Jesus.[11] As with the priesthood and the tabernacle/temple, the tension and relationship between vision on the one hand, and failure on the other, leads us forward into the New Testament presentation of the 'kingship' of the Lord Jesus. The monarchy is such an important feature of the life of Old Testament Israel, and so vital within Old Testament theology, that we need to give it its own chapter. We have a feast in store.

10. See 1 Cor. 3:16; 2 Cor. 6:16; Eph. 2:19-22; Heb. 3:3-6; Rev. 21:22-27.

11. For some quick snapshots here see Luke 1:32-33; Acts 13:32-34; Rom. 1:3-6; Rev. 3:7, 12.

6

The King on the Throne –visions of salvation

1. The start of the monarchy story.

We must begin with the institution of the monarchy under the prophet Samuel. Samuel, you will remember, marks the point of transition from the period of the judges to the era of the monarchy, because it was Samuel, the last judge, who was responsible for appointing Saul, the first king.

The transition was not an easy one. In 1 Samuel 8 the people respond to Samuel's increasingly grey hair by asking for 'a king to judge us like all the nations' (v. 5). In other words, rather than waiting for God to raise up a 'judge' for them as and when they need one—the system operating hitherto, illustrated by Samuel himself—they want a permanent judge, a 'king' who will provide permanent leadership by founding a dynasty.

Samuel is not pleased by the request, and takes his displeasure to the Lord (v. 6):

> And the LORD said to Samuel, 'Obey the voice of the people in all that they say to you, for they have not rejected you, but they have rejected me from being king over them. According to all the deeds that they have done, from the day I brought them up out of

> Egypt even to this day, forsaking me and serving other gods, so they are also doing to you.' (1 Sam. 8:7-8)

So monarchy is not a good idea, it seems. In fact, it is an act of rebellion against God. By rejecting the 'Samuel' model of leadership—a judge raised up as needed, by divine appointment—the people are effectively saying that they do not trust their God to provide for them: they are rejecting *God's* kingship. So Samuel then proceeds to tell them how a king, if they have one, will exploit and oppress them and enrich himself at their expense (vv. 10-18).

But strangely God tells Samuel to go ahead and give them a king nonetheless ('obey the voice of the people', vv. 7, 22). So we then hear about the appointment of Saul, in which Samuel plays a leading positive role (1 Sam. 9-10). Why this strange 'No, it's rebellion—but Yes, it's OK' process?

Old Testament scholarship has made a huge meal of this, arguing that there is a flat contradiction here between positive and negative views of the monarchy—views so sharply opposed (they say), that there must have been different source documents which were woven together to create 1 Samuel as we have it. For instance, Georg Fohrer wrote that the many 'tensions, repetitions, and parallels, the interweaving of various narratives, and the differences between the views or biases expressed' show 'unequivocally' that 1 Samuel is a tissue of contradictory narrative fragments woven together without harmonising, some expressing a positive, and others a negative, view of monarchy.[1]

But it is actually not easy to tease the sections apart into separate 'positive' and 'negative' passages. Just one

---

1. Georg Fohrer, *Introduction to the Old Testament* (trans. David Green; London: SPCK, 1974), p. 217.

illustration of this: the story about Saul's reluctance to be appointed—hiding in a pile of kitbags while the lots are cast to choose the king[2]—falls within one of the 'negative' sections, 1 Samuel 10:17-27. But it makes no sense that Saul should rush off and hide unless he knew that the lot was going to fall on him because Samuel had already anointed him: and *that* story falls within one of the 'positive' sections, 1 Samuel 9:1-10:16. We need 10:1 (his anointing) to explain 10:22 (his hiding while the lots are cast).

No—there is no 'unequivocally' negative view of the monarchy in the Old Testament:[3] only an elderly, conservative, crusty and put-out prophet (Samuel) who receives the request for a king as a rejection of his leadership. In a sense, he is right: the people have indeed rejected God as well as Samuel (see 8:7), because they are not trusting God to raise up the next Samuel for them. 'Theocracy'—direct rule by God—did not mean no human leaders. It meant that, whenever Israel got into a pickle, they could appeal to God their King for help and God would provide a human rescuer, a 'judge'. Now, post-Samuel, they want theocracy to be expressed through the permanent provision of a human 'king'. They want a guarantee that, at every moment, their leader will be there for them.

There is a huge downside to this, as the disgruntled Samuel explains at length.[4] His reaction to their request was partly selfish, partly sour, partly good and partly godly—a very human mix. But being the godly man he was, once he had received the direction from God,

2. 1 Sam. 10:21-23.

3. Fohrer suggests that there was always an 'anti-monarchist' faction in Israel. Certainly, there was criticism of individual kings, but the institution of monarchy itself never seems to have gathered a vocal body of opposition.

4. 1 Sam. 8:10-18.

he could wholeheartedly identify himself with the new thing God was doing.

God underlines to the people (through Samuel) that their king will not be able to save them from 'the curse of the covenant', if they should fall under it[5]—but new and great covenant blessings lie ahead through this appointment, as we will see. God had a bigger vision than just giving the Israelites an additional sense of security—a vision which will take us eventually through to the New Testament conception of the Kingdom of God. And amazingly that bigger vision encompassed the *failure* of the Old Testament monarchy, just like the failure of the other covenant institutions. To trace this story, let's focus next on the underlying purpose, and vision, behind the monarchy.

2. The motivations for the monarchy.

I want to suggest three motivations for monarchy in the Old Testament:

(1) Dissatisfaction with other forms of leadership.

The book of Judges paves the way for the monarchy here. In spite of God's provision of a succession of 'judges', the book named after them traces a terrible decline in the nation's life after Samson (who was himself a truly dreadful judge):

- *In religion:* Micah sets up his own priesthood and temple (Judges 17).
- *In politics:* there is unrest among the tribes, and the tribe of Dan is on the warpath seeking new territory for themselves (Judges 18).
- *In morality:* Judges 19-21 tells the appalling story of the Levite and his concubine, and its aftermath.

5. 1 Sam. 12:13-15, 25.

In relation to each, the repeated verdict of Judges is the same:

> In those days there was no king in Israel. Everyone did what was right in his own eyes.[6]

In fact the final long and dreadful episode in Judges is bracketed around by this comment—notice 19:1 and 21:25. The author of Judges was clearly a monarchic enthusiast, as if to say, 'Well, what do you expect? Without a king, how do you expect religion to be kept on the right tracks, politics to be peaceful, and morality secured?' We should probably date Judges either just before the monarchy, or (perhaps better) during the early honeymoon period when all went swimmingly for Israel under her kings—because, of course, the honeymoon period was very short-lived. Very quickly, things began to fall apart, in all three areas. If 1 Kings 10 gives us the height of the success of the monarchy, describing it through the eyes of the astonished Queen of Sheba, then 1 Kings 11–12 brings us down to earth with a terrible thud, describing Solomon's religious and moral decline and the political collapse of the kingdom under Rehoboam and Jeroboam. Judges could not have been written at that time!

But failure did not (does not) mean the end of hope for something better—far from it. Failure *reinforces* the hope of a king who will truly fulfil the ideal that animated the author of Judges, and displace all other inadequate forms of human leadership.

(2) The need for security in an insecure world.
The second motivation for the monarchy is voiced by the people themselves in their initial demand:

---

6. Judges 17:6: also 18:1, 19:1 and 21:25.

> But the people refused to obey the voice of Samuel. And they said, 'No! But there shall be a king over us, that we also may be like all the nations, and that our king may judge us and go out before us and fight our battles.' (1 Sam. 8:19-20)

Samuel's response is that this is exactly what the judges, raised up by the Lord, had done for them:

> And the LORD sent Jerubbaal and Barak and Jephthah and Samuel and delivered you out of the hand of your enemies on every side, and you lived in safety. But when you saw that Nahash the king of the Ammonites came against you, you said to me, 'No, but a king shall reign over us,' when the LORD your God was your king. (1 Sam. 12:11-12)

The need for security in the face of multiple threats still grips us, both on individual and national levels. Where can we find safety? Of course, the threats to our safety are as big as the shortness of our lifespan and the inevitability of death: we need a King who can save us from death, not just from Nahash and the Ammonites! And that is where the biblical theology of the covenant ends up, offering us a Saviour who 'is able to save to the uttermost those who draw near to God through him'.[7] This longing for security is connected to the third motivation for monarchy in the Old Testament:

(3) Divine mercy towards a desperate people.
Monarchy is a covenant reaction of the same merciful God who saw Israel's plight in Egypt and heard their cry for help:

> Their cry for rescue from slavery came up to God ... 'I have surely seen the affliction of my people who are

7. Heb. 7:25.

in Egypt and have heard their cry … the cry of the people of Israel has come to me …' (Exod. 2:23, 3:7, 9)

Moses began the sequence of judges sent to rescue Israel. But they were not enough. In spite of Samuel's successful rule, the people were still 'crying out' for greater security. So God replaced the old theocracy (expressed through successive judges) with a new theocratic form, which He purposed to bless and to use—in fact, through which He intended to secure His people finally within the covenant blessings all along promised.

The letter to the Hebrews expresses how the Lord Jesus is, for us, precisely what Israel was 'crying out' for, in asking for a king. In a society where there was no developed judicial system and no social security provision for age or disability, the kings (like the judges before them) were the point of reference for people in need or in dispute. They would travel to Jerusalem to present their case before the king[8]—although one man could not deal with everything, a failing Absalom tried to exploit to his own advantage.[9] Psalm 72 expresses beautifully Israel's longing in its prayer for the king, the 'royal son'—

> May he judge your people with righteousness, and your poor with justice! … May he defend the cause of the poor of the people, give deliverance to the children of the needy, and crush the oppressor! (Ps. 72:2, 4)

This lies behind Hebrews' encouragement to us to know that our 'high priest' can sympathise with all our weaknesses; and because our high priest is also a King:

8. See e.g. 2 Sam. 8:15, 14:4-8; 1 Kings 3:16-28.

9. 2 Sam. 15:2-6.

> Let us then with confidence draw near to the throne of grace, that we may receive mercy and find grace to help in time of need. (Heb. 4:16)

Our high-priest-king is truly able to deliver the 'mercy', 'grace' and 'help' we need, and there is no shortage of access to His throne! So *how* was the Israelite monarchy meant to achieve that goal—securing the covenant blessings for Israel? Paradoxically, in order to open this up, we must explore more precisely the *failure* of the monarchy within Israel.

3. The vision of covenant perfection—and its failure. The monarchy was founded on a truly remarkable footing. After its somewhat shaky start under Saul, the monarchy really comes into its own under David, and specifically when God 'reveals his hand' in 2 Samuel 7. He lets Israel (and us) into the secret, and we begin to see His bigger purpose behind His acquiescence with the people's request for a king under Samuel.

Prompted (no doubt) by Deuteronomy 12:1-14, David decides that the time has come to build a proper 'house' for the Lord—a temple in Jerusalem. But the Lord declines the offer, and then wonderfully and meekly tips the idea on its head, and promises instead to build a 'house' for David:

> The LORD declares to you that the LORD will make you a house. When your days are fulfilled and you lie down with your fathers, I will raise up your offspring after you, who shall come from your body, and I will establish … the throne of his kingdom for ever. (2 Sam. 7:11-13)

God promises that David's dynasty will be completely secure:

> When [your son] commits iniquity, I will discipline him with the rod of men, with the stripes of the sons of men, but my steadfast love will not depart from him, as I took it from Saul, whom I put away from before you. And your house and your kingdom shall be made sure for ever before me. Your throne shall be established for ever. (2 Sam. 7:14-16)

This is not just for David's benefit. The whole point of this covenant commitment is to provide security for Israel:

> I will appoint a place for my people Israel and will plant them, so that they may dwell in their own place and be disturbed no more. And violent men shall afflict them no more, as formerly, from the time that I appointed judges over my people Israel. And I will give you rest from all your enemies. (2 Sam. 7:10-11)

So this covenant with David, to create a 'house' for him, is like a glorious codicil on the covenant with Israel: this is *how* Israel will be established securely in the earth. Isaiah later calls it God's 'steadfast, sure love for David', in a passage where he imagines this special 'everlasting covenant' with David being extended to embrace all who respond to the Lord's invitation to 'incline your ear, and come to me; hear, that your soul may live.'[10] It is not a private arrangement just for David's benefit: because he is the king, all under his throne will be blessed by this special monarchic covenant.

The key and characteristic point of this covenant emerges when God says, of David's son yet to succeed him:

> I will be to him a father, and he shall be to me a son. (2 Sam. 7:14)

---

10. Isa. 55:3. The older translation is well known—'the sure mercies of David.'

What a dramatic thing to say, that the son of David will be the son of God! You can see where this is heading, within the wonderful sweep of biblical theology: yes, towards the glorious confession of the Lord Jesus as both Son of David and Son of God[11] (even the great title 'Christ'—the 'anointed one'—points back to the anointing at the heart of coronation[12]), but also towards an even greater blessing than Isaiah was envisaging, namely the *extension* of 'sonship' to cover all who belong under the rule of Jesus the Christ. Here's a little Bible exploration to follow through:

- Compare the promise in 2 Samuel 7:14 (above) with the promises in 2 Corinthians 6:18 and Revelation 21:7.
- Notice how the two New Testament texts are echoing the wording of the covenant promise to David and his descendants.
- Ask *to whom* the promise is being applied in these New Testament texts.
- Draw the biblical conclusion: we *all* become royalty in Jesus Christ, if we belong to Him!

In the Old Testament, the theme of the king as God's Son is particularly opened up in the Psalms.[13] For instance, in that wonderful coronation ode, Psalm 2, we read:

> The LORD said to me, 'You are my Son; today I have begotten you. Ask of me, and I will make the nations your heritage, and the ends of the earth your possession. You shall break them with a rod of

---

11. See e.g. Rom. 1:3-4.

12. See 1 Sam. 10:1, 16:13; 1 Kings 1:39.

13. See the article on 'Messiah' in *The Illustrated Bible Dictionary,* where I devote a paragraph to summarising all the strands of reference to the Messianic King in the Psalms (Leicester: IVP, 1980, pp. 989-90).

iron, and dash them in pieces like a potter's vessel.' (Ps. 2:7-9)

On His coronation day, *this* King (unlike all other kings) is taken into unique relationship with Yahweh, and as Yahweh's Son is given world heritage status: that is, the world *is* His heritage. He has universal rule and power. The greatness of this seems quite extraordinary now, even alarming. It must have seemed almost crazy, at the time. But it makes sense within the covenant theology we have surveyed. Remember that the Lord constituted Israel to be His people by overthrowing the forces of the world. He overthrew Egypt, and brought His people out. He carved a way for them into the land He promised, and no nation could stop them. So when people looked at this Yahweh-king upon His throne, reigning there at Yahweh's right hand, they saw Him implicitly as monarch of the whole earth. Their faith would not allow them to see less, for He reigns as the covenant monarch by virtue of the covenant God who showed His sovereignty over the nations by bringing His people into this kingdom, tiny though it was in comparison with the mighty powers surrounding it.

In comparison with this vision, what a failure the monarchy was! David failed morally,[14] Solomon failed religiously,[15] Rehoboam failed politically,[16] and the kingdom ended up sundered, with the north following a schismatic religion as well as a breakaway king. But in spite of this failure, every new monarch ascending the throne was still greeted with the words of Psalm 2, 'You are my Son …'—while doubtless people were saying under their breath, 'If only you were!' In a real

14. 2 Sam. 11 (cf. 1 Kings 15:5); 2 Sam. 24:17.

15. 1 Kings 11:1-8.

16. 1 Kings 12:16-19.

sense, the words of Psalm 2 could never be true of any of the human occupants of the throne of Israel: even at its greatest extent under Solomon, it was never the case that his kingdom encompassed 'the ends of the earth'. This could only be said *by faith,* and *in anticipation.* We are heading towards the New Testament vision of God's Kingdom truly embracing the whole earth, under the rule of David's most glorious Son, Jesus the Christ.[17]

The vision of this kingship never faded! It was energised, I suggest, by the very failure and inadequacy of the actual human occupants of the throne in Jerusalem. Their failure empowered the development of the vision, for the prophets knew that the Lord must have something even greater in mind, in order to fulfil the covenant promises. If not the human occupants of the throne in Jerusalem, then what?

This question takes us forward into our last chapter together, where we will especially look at the development of the covenant visions surrounding the monarchy and Israel in the prophets.

---

17. Just as a little aside, it's worth noticing how Paul interprets Psalm 2 in his sermon at Antioch in Acts 13: he sees 'you are my Son, today I have begotten you' as fulfilled in the *resurrection* of Jesus—the moment when He rises to universal Lordship (see Acts 2:36)—and says that the resurrection is God's gift of 'the sure mercies of David' as in Isaiah 55:3 (Acts 13:32-34). See also Acts 4:24-28, quoting Ps. 2:1-2.

7

Covenant Visions –the inspiration of hope

I want to suggest four headings under which we can analyse the component parts of the visions surrounding the 'where next' of the covenant, especially in the Psalms and the prophets. The prophets were not put off by the multiple failures hitherto: far from it. Their faith and their vision rose to encompass whole new vistas, new expectations of God's action to fulfil His covenant promises. In four nutshells, what did they see?

Each of these headings uses the word 'perfection', because the prophets expected no less from the fulfilment of the covenant promises. Later, the author of the letter to the Hebrews develops this theme explicitly and lays emphasis on the 'perfection' we can expect when God brings His glorious purposes to their end goal.[1] We'll look a little at Hebrews' development of this theme in a moment.

1. The perfection of monarchy in the person of the divine David.

I'm using the phrase 'divine David' very deliberately here. The Old Testament makes it very clear that the

1. See e.g. Heb. 7:11, 9:9-12, 10:14, 11:39–12:2.

coming King, through whom the covenant promises will be fulfilled, will be a divine figure—though without specifying exactly how this will work. For instance, the royal wedding Psalm (Psalm 45) takes the extraordinary step of addressing the king as 'God':

> Your throne, O God, is for ever and ever. The sceptre of your kingdom is a sceptre of uprightness; you have loved righteousness and hated wickedness. Therefore God, your God, has anointed you with the oil of gladness beyond your companions ... (Ps. 45:6-7)

Some translations tone this down. For instance, the old Revised Standard Version had, 'Your divine throne endures for ever and ever,' making the deity attach (in some vague, unspecified way) to the throne, rather than to the throne's occupant. But this is not what the Hebrew says, as is recognised now by the updated New Revised Standard Version which has, 'Your throne, O God, endures for ever and ever.' The Old Testament is wrestling with a tension which it does not, and indeed cannot, resolve:

- On the one hand, if it takes seriously the covenant promise 'You are my Son,' then it must address its king as God.
- But on the other hand, since the king is manifestly not God, it must make clear that the king lives in an unspecified but uniquely intimate relationship with God, as the Psalm does immediately in verse 7. ('Therefore God, your God, has anointed you with the oil of gladness beyond your companions.')

In spite of this tension, the Old Testament never loses its grip on the divine Messiah. We meet the same thing in Isaiah 9:6-7, where the child to be born is the prince with the fourfold name, 'Wonderful Counsellor, Mighty

God, Everlasting Father, Prince of Peace.' Here too some translations seek to tone down 'Mighty God'—a title used of God Himself just a few paragraphs later[2]—and render it 'Mighty Hero'[3] or 'in battle God-like'.[4] They have been supported by a raft of Old Testament scholars who seek to resist the clear meaning of the Hebrew and argue for something like 'a godlike warrior'. But no—we must take the Bible seriously in what it actually asserts, whether we find it difficult or not: and here there is no doubt about the *deity* of the coming son of David, who will 'increase' the 'government' and 'peace' of His rule without end (9:7).[5] He is 'Warrior God'.[6]

Or what about Jeremiah 23:5-6:

> Behold, the days are coming, declares the LORD, when I will raise up for David a righteous Branch, and he shall reign as king and deal wisely, and shall execute justice and righteousness in the land. In his days Judah will be saved, and Israel will dwell securely. And this is the name by which he will be called: 'The LORD is our righteousness.'

We are familiar with the notion of a 'family tree' with 'branches'. The coming King is descended from David, a branch of his dynasty. But this King is no mere descendant. He will bring wisdom, justice and security through His rule not because He is a particularly good king as kings go, but because of the unique name He bears, greater than any name David could claim. In His

---

2. Isa. 10:21.

3. Revised English Bible.

4. New English Bible.

5. For the detailed evidence see Alec Motyer, *The Prophecy of Isaiah* (Leicester: IVP, 1993), pp. 104-105.

6. This is my translation of the Hebrew phrase, in Alec Motyer, *Isaiah by the Day. A New Devotional Translation* (Fearn: Christian Focus, 2011), p. 57.

very nature He is the righteousness of the Lord, God's action to create justice and salvation for the people He rules.[7]

Or what about Isaiah 11:1-10, another passage depicting the coming son of David, 'a shoot from the stump of Jesse, and a branch from his roots' (v. 1). This 'branch' uniquely possesses 'the Spirit of the LORD' (v. 2) so that He is able to execute perfect justice and righteousness (vv. 3-5), and bring in a complete transformation of the relationships between all animate life (vv. 6-8), such that peace reigns universally and 'the earth shall be full of the knowledge of the LORD as the waters cover the sea' (v. 9). In fact this 'branch' of Jesse is really Jesse's 'root'—the source and foundation of the whole dynasty—bringing in universal rule (v. 10, and look on to vv. 11-12).

And what about Isaiah 52:7-12, the passage that leads in to the famous fourth servant-song, Isaiah 53, to which we turn next. When the Servant comes He will be 'the arm of the LORD'—God Himself rolling up His sleeves to save His people (53:1). This is because the coming of the Servant is announced by a herald who proclaims 'the return of the LORD to Zion' (52:8). *The Lord Himself* is coming to His people, because 'the LORD has bared his holy arm before the eyes of all the nations, and all the ends of the earth shall see the salvation of our God' (52:10). David's universal rule, potential but never actual under Israel's kings, will be realised when the Lord Himself arrives in Zion to bring salvation to the whole earth.

This is the glorious vision of the *outcome* of the covenant with Israel: a vision which of course feeds into and underlies the New Testament conception of

---

7. cf. Rom. 3:21-22; 2 Cor. 5:21.

the Kingdom of God. Our next headings unpack some of the details and focuses of this salvation.

2. The perfection of priesthood in 'the Servant of the Lord'.

Let's look more closely at Isaiah 53. One of the keys to understanding this most important poem about the coming ministry of God's 'Servant' is to notice the ways in which its themes are picked up and celebrated in the following chapter, Isaiah 54. In particular, let me draw out three themes which emerge in this way, all of them central covenant themes, and all of them looking forward to the coming fulfilment of the covenant vision:

1. Miraculous children, new family.

The theme of 'children' runs through Isaiah 54, starting with the amazing invitation to 'the barren' to break into song:

> 'Sing, O barren one, who did not bear; break forth into singing and cry aloud, you who have not been in labour! For the children of the desolate one will be more than the children of her who is married,' says the LORD. (Isa. 54:1)

These miraculous new children, born to the barren, will spearhead a new worldwide kingdom ('your offspring will possess the nations,' v. 3) and an end to shame (v. 4), and all because:

> Your Maker is your husband, the LORD of hosts is his name; and the Holy One of Israel is your Redeemer, the God of the whole earth he is called. (Isa. 54:5)

The Lord is bringing to birth a whole new, worldwide family. How have these miracle-children come to be? The answer lies back in 53:10:

> When his soul makes an offering for sin, he shall see his offspring; he shall prolong his days; the will of the LORD shall prosper in his hands.

Part of the Lord's will for His Servant is that, through offering Himself as a sacrifice for sin, He should bring to birth new 'offspring'. Isaiah 54 unpacks this a little more, but does not explain the mystery of this new birth—this creation, in fact, of a new people born by other-than-human means. We have to wait for John 1:12-13 and 3:3-8 to learn more of what this means!

2. An end to fear, new peace.

These new children are going to enjoy the Lord's *shalom:*

> All your children shall be taught by the LORD, and great shall be the peace of your children. In righteousness you shall be established; you shall be far from oppression, for you shall not fear; and from terror, for it shall not come near you. (Isa. 54:13-14)

Paul unpacks these themes beautifully in Romans 5:1-5.[8] Here in Isaiah, if we ask for the source of this peace, we find it in 53:5:

> But he was wounded for our transgressions; he was crushed for our iniquities; upon him was the chastisement that brought us peace, and with his stripes we are healed.

This new peace arises directly out of the sacrificial, substitutionary suffering of the Servant on our behalf. In chapter 54 Isaiah wants to assure us that this peace is solid, sure and lasting:

> 'For the mountains may depart and the hills be removed, but my steadfast love shall not depart from you, and

8. Note also how the first phrase here ('all your children shall be taught by the LORD') is quoted by Jesus in John 6:45: this is fulfilled as people respond in faith to Jesus and listen to His teaching.

> my covenant of peace shall not be removed,' says the LORD, who has compassion on you. (Isa. 54:10)

By using the word 'covenant' to describe this glorious promise, the Lord links this assurance to the covenant with Israel, which takes us right back to Noah and Abraham. This is where it has all been heading!—towards an absolutely unshakeable, worldwide *shalom* shared by God and His people, based on His compassion and secured by His 'steadfast love'. Passages like this were prompting Paul when he wrote Romans 8:31-39 to assure us that nothing in all creation (and he lists some powerful candidates) 'will be able to separate us from the love of God in Christ Jesus our Lord.'[9] In the Lord Jesus this 'covenant of peace' becomes a lived reality for all who belong to Him.

That leads us to the third theme in Isaiah 54 which draws on and develops the picture of the ministry of God's servant in Isaiah 53:

3. Impregnable security, new righteousness.

The word 'righteousness' occurs twice in Isaiah 54, first in verse 14 ('In righteousness you shall be established …'), then again in verse 17 where the ESV translates it 'vindication'. Let's retranslate verse 17:

> Not a single tool fashioned against you will flourish! and every tongue which rises to bring a case against you will prove guilty. This is the possession of the servants of Yahweh, and their righteousness is straight from me. This is the word of Yahweh.[10]

This too seems to lie behind Romans 8:31-39—see especially Paul's assurance, 'Who shall bring any charge against God's elect? It is God who justifies. Who is to

9. Rom. 8:39.

10. This is the translation in *Isaiah by the Day,* p. 264.

condemn?'[11] Again, this theme of 'righteousness' arises from Isaiah 53—and in fact Paul's whole doctrine of 'justification' is very possibly deeply influenced by Isaiah 53:11:

> Out of the anguish of his soul he shall see and be satisfied; by his knowledge shall the righteous one, my servant, make many to be accounted righteous, and he shall bear their iniquities.

—or, more exactly, he will 'provide righteousness for the many'.[12] Paul echoes this verse in Romans 5:18-19, as he unpacks the 'act of obedience' by which the Lord Jesus achieved righteousness/justification for us. What is this 'righteousness'? Both in Isaiah and in Paul it means 'right standing', being in a 'right' relationship with someone, all offences dealt with and breaches repaired, and a new relationship of love established. The Servant 'provides' this righteousness. The 'and' which follows ('and he shall bear their iniquities') introduces an explanation of this provision of righteousness: this is *how* He brings 'the many' into right relationship with God—He undertakes a priestly work of substitution, being Himself 'wounded for our transgressions … crushed for our iniquities' (v. 5). Here the word 'for' describes an effect arising from a cause, perhaps better translated 'because of'. Our transgressions were the cause of His wounding—all the transgression on our side, all the penalty on His. And as a result we are 'provided with' an unshakeable righteousness before God, a right standing which can never be taken away from us.

---

11. Rom. 8:33-34. 'Justify' and 'make righteous' are both possible translations of the Greek word, just as 'righteousness' and 'vindication' are both good renderings of the Hebrew word (depending on context).

12. This is the translation in *Isaiah by the Day*, p. 260.

This is the priestly work of the servant of God, doing precisely what the lamb did in Egypt, standing in for God's people. And out of this priestly work there comes an 'imputed' righteousness, children who are born without human agency, a covenant of peace which will never be undone.

Who is this Servant who offers Himself in this way to save God's people? Quite simply He is 'the arm of the LORD' (53:1), that is, Yahweh Himself come to take personal action. As we noted above, in the Servant 'the LORD has bared his holy arm' (52:10), rolled His sleeves up and gone into action *Himself* to perform this tremendous work of substitution and priestly offering, through which God's people, supernaturally born, inherit a covenant of peace and are established in righteousness.

3. The perfection of regeneration by a final dealing with sin.

Moses foresaw it all—the problem, the result, the remedy and the restoration. Let's go back to Deuteronomy 30:

> And when all these things come upon you, the blessing and the curse, which I have set before you, and you call them to mind among all the nations where the LORD your God has driven you, and return to the LORD your God, you and your children, and obey his voice in all that I command you today, with all your heart and with all your soul, then the LORD your God will restore your fortunes and have compassion on you, and he will gather you again ... And the LORD your God will circumcise your heart and the heart of your offspring, so that you will love the LORD your God with all your heart and with all your soul, that you may live. (Deut. 30:1-3, 6)

- The problem—the uncircumcised, disobedient heart.
- The result—the 'curses' of the covenant, in particular expulsion from the land God gave.
- The remedy—the circumcision of the disobedient heart, so that heart-felt love and obedience follow.
- The restoration—physically, re-gathering to the land (v. 3); spiritually, an entry into true love and life (v. 6).

This is what Isaiah has in mind when he writes of the people being established in righteousness. But it fell to Jeremiah to be the one to spell out this future perfection in the fullest Old Testament detail—in his great 'new covenant' chapter, Jeremiah 31:

> Behold, the days are coming, declares the LORD, when I will make a new covenant with the house of Israel and the house of Judah, not like the covenant that I made with their fathers on the day when I took them by the hand to bring them out of the land of Egypt, my covenant that they broke, though I was their husband, declares the LORD. But this is the covenant that I will make with the house of Israel after those days, declares the LORD: I will put my law within them, and I will write it on their hearts. And I will be their God, and they shall be my people. And no longer shall each one teach his neighbour and each his brother, saying, 'Know the LORD,' for they shall all know me, from the least of them to the greatest, declares the LORD. For I will forgive their iniquity, and I will remember their sin no more. (Jer. 31:31-34)

It's worth quoting this passage at length, because this is exactly what the author of Hebrews does: he quotes this entire passage in Hebrews 8:8-12, thus giving us the longest single quotation from the Old Testament in the New. This illustrates how vital is this theme of the 'new covenant'—and covenant theology generally—both within Hebrews, and within the New Testament. Hebrews' immediate conclusion, after this quotation, is very telling:

> In speaking of a new covenant, he makes the first one obsolete. And what is becoming obsolete and growing old is ready to vanish away. (Heb. 8:13)

The old covenant, as we've seen, was fatally flawed. It simply could not bring home the bacon—that is, actually deliver the promises at its heart. Through Jeremiah, God promises to take action to remedy this: and Hebrews rejoices that this is precisely what God has done, through Jesus Christ. Look closely at what Jeremiah says in this passage:

- The new covenant arises, like the old, from that 'Passover moment' when God launched His people on a journey with Him out of Egypt, by providing a lamb to stand in their place.
- BUT Israel 'broke' that original covenant: we've traced the sad story of this 'breaking'.
- Yet God does not abandon His commitment to His people—He is still their 'husband' (v. 32). The covenant is unbroken in *God's* hands, and so
- He acts to mend the problem, not by lowering the bar and reducing the obligation, but by raising *us* so that we can meet it. To achieve this He does two things, closely interlinked:

  1. He changes our hearts, writing His law within us, so that we don't have to learn laboriously to obey Him, but it is the *instinct* of all God's people to 'know' Him (v. 34). He gifts a new nature.

2. And the root of it all: as in Isaiah, the creation of this regenerate people arises from a final dealing with sin: 'I will forgive their iniquity, and I will remember their sin no more.'

- As a result, the great covenant aim is fulfilled: 'I will be their God, and they shall be my people' (v. 33). The relationship is secure, all threat removed.

When God forgets our sin, it is truly finished. If it is no longer held in the divine memory, then it is truly as if it had never been, vanishing like morning mist in the glory of the victorious grace that brings the covenant people home. Hebrews unpacks the long quotation of Jeremiah 31 over the two chapters which follow it, and draws the conclusion:

> For by a single offering he has perfected for all time those who are being sanctified (Heb. 10:14)

That's you and me! We experience a process of 'being sanctified' through all the ups and downs of life, as the new heart and mind is formed in us through the work of the Holy Spirit, and we learn to love and obey Him better.[13] But from God's perspective, we 'have been perfected'—the job is already done! —because Jesus' offering of Himself is the sacrifice to end all sacrifices: 'Where there is forgiveness of sins, there is no longer any offering for sin' (Heb. 10:18). Nothing more is needed to secure the covenant. Perfected through Him, we are safe 'for all time'.

---

13. See also Rom. 5:5; also Rom. 2:15, 29; 2 Cor. 3:3; Eph. 4:23-24; Luke 22:20; 1 Cor. 11:25—all passages which reflect or echo Jeremiah's 'new covenant' prophecy.

4. The perfection of divine indwelling secured by princely mediation.

We round off our tracing of the Old Testament covenant story in the prophecy of Ezekiel. As we've seen, the whole focus of the covenant promise is summarised in God's commitment 'to be God to you and to your offspring after you' (Gen. 17:7—picked up, as we just saw, in Jeremiah's new covenant prophecy). The prophets knew that God had not abandoned His commitment to make this a reality, in spite of Israel's sinful rebellion against Him. At the heart of it was God's desire to 'dwell' in the midst of His people—to be God to them not at a distance, but in intimate relationship and, as we've seen, this desire for *closeness* to His people motivated the great covenant institutions, especially the tabernacle and the temple.

There was frustration about it, too: on the one hand the tabernacle/temple, the dwelling of God Himself, was right among the people; but on the other hand, God dwelt there in splendid isolation, and the people were kept back from direct contact because of their uncleanness and sinfulness. Only the High Priest was allowed into the Most Holy Place, and that only once a year, on the Day of Atonement. Otherwise, no contact—even though this was the key covenant aim.

Ezekiel picks up this failure of the tabernacle/temple and, in the magnificent extended vision with which his prophecy ends, says that God is going to set this right. We must start in chapter 36, where Ezekiel echoes Jeremiah:

> And I will give you a new heart, and a new spirit I will put within you. And I will remove the heart of stone from your flesh and give you a heart of flesh. And I will put my Spirit within you, and cause you to

> walk in my statutes and be careful to obey my rules. You shall dwell in the land that I gave to your fathers, and you shall be my people, and I will be your God. (Ezek. 36:26-28)

Notice what Ezekiel adds to Jeremiah's vision of the transformed heart: this will be achieved through the gift of 'my Spirit' to indwell God's people—thus enabling, at one stroke, *both* our inner transformation *and* the dwelling of God Himself with(in) His people. What a move, what a dramatic shift! The Spirit of God, previously given just to kings and prophets, will rest on *all* God's people, changing them fundamentally. This glorious prophecy is followed immediately by Ezekiel's famous 'Valley of Dry Bones' vision, which pictures the prophecy of Ezekiel 36 being fulfilled: Israel is raised dramatically from death to new life by the wind of God's Spirit, and restored back to their land from exile. The LORD's comment is:

> And you shall know that I am the LORD, when I open your graves, and raise you from your graves, O my people. And I will put my Spirit within you, and you shall live, and I will place you in your own land. Then you shall know that I am the LORD; I have spoken, and I will do it, declares the LORD. (Ezek. 37:13-14)

Do you notice the same two-sided restoration that we observed in Moses' prophecy in Deuteronomy 30?—to the *land* and to the *Lord*, physical and spiritual hand in hand.

Ezekiel then prophesies that Israel and Judah will be reunited in the land, the hateful division a thing of the past, under the rule of a single king:

> My servant David shall be king over them, and they shall all have one shepherd. They shall walk in my rules and be careful to obey my statutes. They shall

> dwell in the land that I gave to my servant Jacob, where your fathers lived. They and their children and their children's children shall dwell there for ever, and David my servant shall be their prince for ever. I will make a covenant of peace with them. And I will set them in their land and multiply them, and I will set my sanctuary in their midst for evermore. My dwelling-place shall be with them, and I will be their God, and they shall be my people. Then the nations will know that I am the LORD who sanctifies Israel, when my sanctuary is in their midst for evermore. (Ezek. 37:24-28)

Ezekiel's temple passage in chapters 40–48 then sets out the details of this dwelling in the land under a new 'covenant of peace' mediated by the 'prince' who is their 'shepherd'. Ezekiel, you will remember, was prophesying during the exile, after the destruction of Jerusalem and the temple by the Babylonians, and before the restoration and rebuilding which began after Cyrus the King of Persia allowed the exiled Israelites to return.[14] Looking ahead, Ezekiel sets out a visionary blueprint for the restoration, arising from his expectation of Israel's regeneration by the Spirit. The 'returnees' quite rightly never sought to turn his blueprint into literal plans: Ezekiel didn't want to *prescribe* the rebuilding for them, but to *inspire* it with a vision of *God's* priorities. He can inspire us in the same way, especially because we can see where it was all heading, as God's plans for the regeneration of His people unfold in the New Testament.

In sum, Ezekiel's temple vision is a spelling out, at length, of the reality, the security and the blessings that ensue when God perfectly tabernacles in the midst of

14. See Ezra 1–2. The destruction of the city and temple took place in 586B.C., and the return recorded by Ezra took place in 538B.C.

His people. Let me set out for you three key elements of the vision:

(1) Symbolic redistribution of the land.

Ezekiel gives exact measurements for a symbolic redivision of the land between the tribes of Israel.[15] The change from the previous division under Joshua[16] says clearly: this is a whole new start, a recreated people! And the shape of the redistribution expresses the theology underlying this new 'covenant of peace': the temple sits right at the heart of the land, surrounded by the territory apportioned to 'the prince', with the tribes of Israel placed around the prince, so that the prince mediates between the people and the temple. This dramatic reshaping of Israel's whole existence is signalled even by a new name for Jerusalem:

> And the name of the city from that time on shall be, The LORD is there. (Ezek. 48:35)

This prophecy, the very last words of Ezekiel, gives us the absolutely key idea: he is not hidden in the sanctuary at the heart of the city, but the whole city is now his dwelling—and his people share it with him.

(2) Symbolic reconstruction of the cult.

This geographical mediation reflects the mediatorial role of the prince, who is clearly also a priest:

> It shall be the prince's duty to furnish the burnt offerings, grain offerings, and drink offerings, at the feasts, the new moons, and the Sabbaths, all the appointed feasts of the house of Israel: he shall provide the sin offerings, grain offerings, burnt offerings, and peace offerings, to make atonement on behalf of the house of Israel. (Ezek. 45:17)

---

15. Ezek. 45:1-8, 47:13–48:29.
16. Josh. 13:8–19:48.

The Davidic kings, reigning in Jerusalem, were regarded as having a *priestly* as well as a royal role,[17] but they never supplied all offerings for all worshippers! What a wonderful and dramatic foreshadowing of the great 'prince', the coming Son of David, who will offer (as the *Book of Common Prayer* so memorably puts it) 'a full, perfect and sufficient sacrifice, oblation and satisfaction for the sins of the whole world.' *He* does all the offering, we do all the receiving.

But we are not left without any role. In Ezekiel's vision the prince provided all the offerings for the festivals and the Sabbaths, but the repeated daily sacrifices were to be provided by the people—daily reminders and appropriations of the great offerings made by the prince, securing atonement for Israel. So we too, as Paul puts it, must 'present [our] bodies as a living sacrifice, holy and acceptable to God'[18] on the *basis* of the single sufficient sacrifice for sin offered by our Lord Jesus.

Ezekiel imagines a completely reconstructed temple—new dimensions (meticulously described),[19] and new sacrificial arrangements.[20] He sees the glory of the LORD settling on the new temple,[21] as on Solomon's temple. But, whereas earlier the arrival of the Glory meant that even the priests could not enter,[22] now there are no restrictions:

> When the people of the land come before the LORD at the appointed feasts, he who enters by the north gate to worship shall go out by the south gate, and he

---

17. This is especially clear in the case of Solomon: see 1 Kings 8:62, 9:25. In David's case, 2 Sam. 24:25.

18. Rom. 12:1.

19. Ezek. 40–42.

20. Ezek. 43:13–44:31.

21. Ezek. 43:1-9.

22. See Exod. 40:35; 1 Kings 8:10-11.

> who enters by the south gate shall go out by the north gate: no one shall return by way of the gate by which he entered, but each shall go out straight ahead. When they enter, the prince shall enter with them, and when they go out, he shall go out. (Ezek. 46:9-10)

This wonderful prince ensures confident 'access into this grace in which we stand'.[23] As Hebrews puts it, we now

> have confidence to enter the holy places by the blood of Jesus, by the new and living way that he opened for us through the curtain, that is, through his flesh. (Heb. 10:19-20)

As in Ezekiel's vision, our great Prince accompanies us all the way into God's presence (and out again, into the world), enabling restriction-free access.

(3) Symbolic new life for the world.
The vision of the water flowing from the temple in Ezekiel 47:1-12 is truly dramatic. Although these final visions all spring from Ezekiel's expectation of the renewal of God's people by the gift of the Spirit (Ezek. 36:27 and 37:1-14), Ezekiel does not mention the Spirit in this description of the ever-widening flood of water from the altar that brings new life to the desert and to the Dead Sea. But we could regard this vision of new life as forming a pair with the vision of the valley of Dry Bones. God is at work! The Creator God is on the move by His Spirit, summoning life out of death and fruitfulness out of the desert, and this new life spreads irresistibly eastward, out from the renewed Israel into the world. When Isaiah uses the same image, he makes the connection with the Spirit explicit[24]—and of course

23. Rom. 5:2.

24. Isa. 44:3-4.

Jesus also uses 'water' as a picture of the Holy Spirit. In fact, His famous words in John 7:38—

> Whoever believes in me, as the Scripture has said, 'Out of his heart will flow rivers of living water'—

probably draws in part on Ezekiel 47. John's immediate comment is, 'Now this he said about the Spirit, whom those who believed in him were to receive.' When we receive the life-giving water of the Spirit through faith in Christ, we are bathing in Ezekiel's stream, because Jesus is Himself the temple from which the water flows.[25] And like Ezekiel, we can climb onto the bank (47:6) and enjoy the trees growing constantly there to provide never-failing food and healing (47:12). Ultimately this is the river which graces the heavenly city, and that is where we will finally enjoy it!

> Then the angel showed me the river of the water of life, bright as crystal, flowing from the throne of God and of the Lamb through the middle of the street of the city; also, on either side of the river, the tree of life with its twelve kinds of fruit, yielding its fruit each month. The leaves of the tree were for the healing of the nations. (Rev. 22:1-2)

So our survey of Old Testament Covenant Theology brings us to a point of glorious expectation. We are dealing with a God who *never gives up:* despite all opposition, He will not fail to deliver His promises and to rescue His people, ultimately bringing them home to glory with Himself. The story that begins in Eden with the call—and fall—of the first human pair ends in the heavenly Jerusalem beside the same tree of life whose fruit is now freely available to all.[26] In between,

---

25. See John 2:19-22.

26. See Gen. 2:9, 3:22.

the story focuses chiefly on the Lord Jesus as the One through whom God achieves His covenant purposes, but we cannot truly understand what Jesus has done for us unless we trace the winding covenant path that leads us through the Old Testament: from Noah to Abraham, through Moses, David and the prophets who, as Peter puts it, 'prophesied about the grace that was to be yours'.[27]

The grace that is now ours: grace to *experience* and to *understand* the lengths to which God has gone to make real His covenant promise of 'steadfast love' to those who trust in Him.

27. 1 Pet. 1:10.

Editor's Postscript (Steve Motyer)

I was a fresh-faced student when I attended the Theological Students' Fellowship conference (I think at Swanwick) in January 1973, and listened to my father giving four lectures on 'Old Testament Covenant Theology'. Subsequently some bright spark transcribed the lectures from the tape-recordings, printed them off and put copies on sale for 20p. To be honest, I had forgotten that I was at the conference until I discovered that I had my own tape-recordings of the lectures sitting in the loft! But I had a couple of copies of the 20p print-off and so knew immediately what was being referred to, when—at Sinclair Ferguson's suggestion—Christian Focus asked if I would like to prepare the lectures for 'proper' publication. I was delighted to do this, and it has been a great joy to work on them.

In January 1973 my father had been teaching Old Testament to theological students (mostly preparing for Anglican ministry) for nearly twenty years, and just a year before had become the first Principal of Trinity College Bristol, newly formed out of the amalgamation of three Anglican Colleges in Bristol. He already had a well-established reputation as a preacher and teacher, and I believe that he would have responded very readily indeed to the invitation to give these lectures: for 'covenant' was a theme very dear to his heart, often featuring (in different ways) in his preaching, and very definitely in his praying. Towards the end of his life, whenever he came to stay with us, we would ask him to pray at the end of the day before we all set off for bed. Suddenly heaven would open as he prayed, and it was always the great covenant truths of God's faithfulness and steadfast love, our security in Him, the trustworthiness of His promises, and the proof and final expression of this in the cross—these were the truths that lifted him (and us) at the end of each day.

For him, the covenant was at the root of true believing. As he prayed for his family, one of his favourite resting-places was Peter's words at Pentecost, offering forgiveness and the gift of the Holy Spirit to all who repented and were baptised, for (said Peter) 'the promise is for you and for your children and for all who are far off, everyone whom the Lord our God calls to himself' (Acts 2:39). My father rejoiced in the thought that we, his children, were the proper recipients of 'the promise'—signalled (for him) in our baptism as infants—and he prayed that, in line with His promise, the Lord would call us and draw us and help us to *know* the greatness of the covenant blessings in Christ. He would often seek to encourage Christian parents with the thought that, on the basis of the covenant, they can entrust their children into God's keeping, because of His promise. This is a thought that inspires me too.

My father did not like the spoken word in print. He thought that the natural rhetoric employed by speakers—of which he was such a master—did not read well on the page. When he did the same thing (turn recordings of his talks into books) they often ended up completely re-written, because he was so keen to present the ideas well in print. I'm thinking particularly of his beautiful little book *Loving the Old Testament,* which started as three talks at 'Bible By The Beach' in Eastbourne in 2012, and ended up as a mini-book with fourteen chapters (and a lovely Foreword by Tim Keller).[1]

I haven't attempted such a dramatic rewrite! But I've tried to respect what he would have done to these lectures, had he lived to do the job himself. The four lectures have become seven chapters. They have been completely rewritten, though I have basically followed the structure of the lectures, have often used his same headings, and have completely respected his content. But (a) I've toned down a little the specific 'Old Testament scholarship' elements of the lectures (he was

---

1. Alec Motyer, *A Christian's Pocket Guide to Loving the Old Testament. One Book, One God, One Story* (Fearn: Christian Focus, 2015)

talking to theological students, after all), and (b) I have widened the 'whole Bible' element, looking onward to the New Testament more than he does in the original talks. He would certainly have wanted to do this, given more space and a wider readership!

In addition, because at times he was clearly pressed for time, I've done my best to expand some very compressed sections in ways which I hope he would have liked. The most obvious of these is the last section on Ezekiel (barely half a page in the original typescript!)—though here I had some help from his lovely introduction to the Old Testament, *Roots: Let the Old Testament Speak*.[2]

He loved communicating biblical truth to 'ordinary' believers (not that there are such creatures). And one of his lifelong emphases was to encourage personal Bible study—getting to grips with the text for oneself. One of the elements of the lectures that has dropped out is the several points where he encouraged us students to take up various points in our own study. For instance, at one point he encouraged us to grab Young's *Analytical Concordance* and do our own study of the expressions 'atonement' and 'make atonement'. Broad-brush treatments of biblical themes are all very well, but they have to be based on patient and (he would emphasise) *daily* study of the Bible, especially of the precise *words* of the Bible: and he wanted *all* believers—however 'ordinary'—to develop this discipline, not just theological students.

So his final word to us all would be: *become a Bible-lover.* For those who love the Bible cannot fail to fall in love with the God of the Bible, who commits Himself to us in covenant love and shows that love in Jesus Christ our Lord.

---

2. Alec Motyer, *Roots: Let the Old Testament Speak* (edited by John Stott; Fearn: Christian Focus, 2009. First published by Candle Books, 2001).

Christian Focus Publications

Our mission statement –

STAYING FAITHFUL

In dependence upon God we seek to impact the world through literature faithful to His infallible Word, the Bible. Our aim is to ensure that the Lord Jesus Christ is presented as the only hope to obtain forgiveness of sin, live a useful life and look forward to heaven with Him.

Our books are published in four imprints:

CHRISTIAN FOCUS

Popular works including biographies, commentaries, basic doctrine and Christian living.

CHRISTIAN HERITAGE

Books representing some of the best material from the rich heritage of the church.

MENTOR

Books written at a level suitable for Bible College and seminary students, pastors, and other serious readers. The imprint includes commentaries, doctrinal studies, examination of current issues and church history.

CF4•K

Children's books for quality Bible teaching and for all age groups: Sunday school curriculum, puzzle and activity books; personal and family devotional titles, biographies and inspirational stories – because you are never too young to know Jesus!

Christian Focus Publications Ltd,
Geanies House, Fearn, Ross-shire,
IV20 1TW, Scotland, United Kingdom.
www.christianfocus.com